Field Guide to Upland Birds and Waterfowl™

Field Guide to Upland Birds and Waterfowl™

Written and Illustrated by
Christopher S. Smith

Wilderness Adventures Press™

Belgrade, Montana

Maps, book design and cover design © 2000 Wilderness Adventures Press

Published by Wilderness Adventures Press
45 Buckskin Road
Belgrade, MT 59714
800-925-3339
Website: www.wildadv.com
email: books@wildadv.com

10 9 8 7 6 5 4 3 2

Printed in Singapore

Library of Congress Cataloging in Publication Data:

Smith, Christopher S., 1972–
    Field guide to upland birds and waterfowl / written and illustrated by
Christopher S. Smith.
        p.   cm.
    ISBN 1-885106-20-3   (alk. paper)
    1. Upland game birds––North America––Identification.   2. Waterfowl––
North America––Identification.   I. Title.
QL681.S64   2000
598.6'097––dc21   00-033411
                                                                          CIP

Dedication

To Jake,
It's been one of the greatest pleasures to see you take to
the outdoors the way you have…and to be your brother.

To Mags, my constant shadow.
You and I sort of learned the ropes together. I'll miss you.

Table of Contents

Acknowledgements

THIS BOOK HAS BEEN IN THE WORKS for several years now, and a number of people have been more help to me than a mere few sentences can explain. Two outstanding wildlife photographers, John Schafer and Ben Williams, have provided an abundant supply of their duck, goose, and upland bird photographs to use for source material, without which many of the color plates in here would have been impossible.

Tom Alan, Ph.D., ornithologist, and good friend, was kind enough to critique the plates for accuracy. A special thanks also goes to Bob and Bonnie, my dear friends on the Canadian prairie, who have welcomed me and my semitrained Lab every October for the past several years to come photograph the "grand passage" and run around with the ducks and geese for a while. I feel like such a part of the family that I fear they might put me to work on the farm one of these years.

This book would never have gotten far without my brother, Jason, and my father, Steve Smith. I've been blessed with being the brother and son of two writers and biologists, and they willingly donated their knowledge and what sanity they had left to science by editing this book. I've been tagging along with Dad since I was six, carrying a bird book and BB gun—everything in here is a result of the opportunities he gave me.

And my wife, Lani: I've been so fortunate to have you to lean on and keep me pointed in the right direction. You've been a tremendous sport, reacquainting yourself with me in between duck, turkey, goose, and grouse seasons. You pretended to be sleeping as I stumbled out of bed too early, too loud, and too often to "gather research." Autumn is sweeter with you here, and I love you.

Introduction

WHETHER YOU ARE AN ARDENT bird watcher or avid hunter, proper bird identification plays an important role. For birders, bird watching isn't satisfying unless you know what bird you are observing. And for hunters, shooting at a bird you can't identify is out of the question.

For those of you who have not spent much time observing these birds or reading about them, this book should provide a great introduction to the world of waterfowl and upland birds. For those of you who have been hunting a long time but still struggle with the differences between a prairie chicken and sharptail, a lesser and greater scaup, or a gadwall and wigeon, this book should help to sharpen your identification skills. The guide is based on my hunting and bird watching experiences over the years, but more importantly, my extensive scientific education in bird identification. The pocket size is ideal for taking into the field. With all the gear we lug out there, a small pocket guide that provides valuable information to help identify what we're looking at should be with us on all our forays. It's perfect for the glovebox, gamebag, backpack, or back pocket.

How To Use the Guide

Because I like things simple when in the field, I have made this guide easy to use. Diagrams in the front of the two sections illustrate upland bird and waterfowl anatomy, including wings, so that specific terminology referred to in the text will be only a few pages away. After only several uses, you'll recognize the leading edge, the nape, the scapulars, and a host of other bird-related terms without having to refer to these illustrations. Information about waterfowl and upland birds precedes each section. In the waterfowl section, birds are divided into puddle ducks, diving ducks, geese and swans, and other birds.

The first key to knowing the identity of these birds is to know which ones could potentially be in your geographic location. If you're in North Dakota,

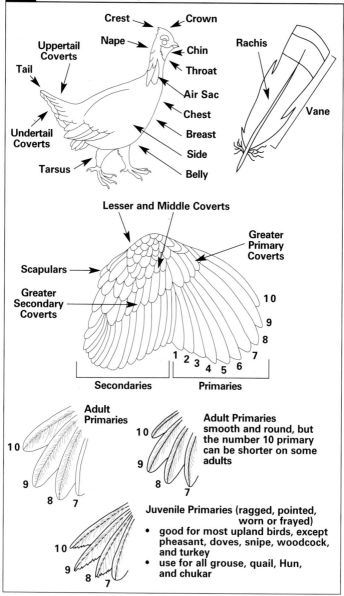

Crest
Crown
Uppertail Coverts
Nape
Chin
Tail
Throat
Air Sac
Chest
Breast
Undertail Coverts
Side
Tarsus
Belly

Rachis
Vane

Lesser and Middle Coverts

Greater Primary Coverts

Scapulars

Greater Secondary Coverts

10
9
8
7

1 2 3 4 5 6

Secondaries

Primaries

Adult Primaries

10
9
8
7

Adult Primaries smooth and round, but the number 10 primary can be shorter on some adults

10
9
8
7

Juvenile Primaries (ragged, pointed, worn or frayed)
• good for most upland birds, except pheasant, doves, snipe, woodcock, and turkey
• use for all grouse, quail, Hun, and chukar

Upland Birds

THE UPLAND GAME BIRDS OF NORTH AMERICA are comprised almost entirely from the order *Galliformes*, meaning "chicken-like" birds, which, of course, includes the most well known of the order, the domestic chicken. All but four of the birds covered in this section—mourning dove, white-winged dove, American woodcock, and common snipe—are *Galliformes* members.

Characteristics that distinguish this bird include: They are terrestrial, meaning they live on land rather than water; they do not swim; their bills are short and stout, which helps in breaking and eating seeds and grains; their legs are short (often spurred among males) and strong, with tough nails to aid in scratching for food and grit; their wings are elliptically-shaped to aid flight in dense surroundings.

The other birds in this section—doves, woodcock, and snipe—have obvious differences from the *Galliformes*. Doves have narrow, pointed wings and a long, thin bill. The woodcock has elliptical wings that aid in flying through dense stands of aspen and alder and, along with the snipe, has a long bill and feet, as do the other shorebirds in this group. Still, these birds are hunted and are therefore considered game birds.

Game birds are noticeably different than most of the waterfowl world in plumage alone. Almost all of the ducks (not geese) covered in this book are sexually dimorphic (obvious visual differences between male and female). Game birds, on the other hand, vary by species. Some are sexually dimorphic, while others are sexually monomorphic (not obviously different visually). Sexing is still possible with monomorphic birds, and methods to sex each bird are included in the text facing each color plate. However, some species can be quite subjective, and you will only become good at differentiating the sexes with practice.

The ring-necked pheasant is the most common sexually dimorphic game bird. It is the only game bird, other than the turkey, that has specific hunting restrictions requiring that no females can be shot (except on preserves or during some fall turkey hunting seasons). For all other game birds, even if dimorphic, such as the northern bobwhite quail, both sexes are legal targets.

This is mainly because of the amount of time it would take to locate and pick a male from a flock of birds flushing in chaos and thick cover—it would make hunting them next to impossible. Monomorphic game birds include the chukar, gray partridge, some species of grouse and ptarmigan, snipe, woodcock, and mountain and scaled quail. Once in hand, some of the sexual differences are easy to see, but unless the birds hold still or are in courtship display, it can be difficult to tell from a distance.

Aging game birds is also difficult, especially at first. A number of methods have been devised to make an educated guess when birds are distant, but most often, aging cannot be done unless the bird is in hand. One of the most universal ways to make an accurate guess at the age of game birds is to observe the outer primary feathers, specifically primaries 8, 9, and 10. Some species, such as pheasant, woodcock, and snipe, are excluded from this procedure.

Upland birds molt during the summer, growing in new feathers to replace those that have become damaged due to the beating and everyday wear and tear that occurs over a year. When a bird molts its primary feathers, it begins with the innermost primary, number 1, and works outward to number 10. Adult male birds begin molting these feathers while young (immature or juvenile) birds are still growing. Adult females do not molt with adult males because they can't afford to expend the energy necessary for feather replacement due to the demands of egg laying, incubation, and protection of young birds. Females molt later in the year, at the time that juveniles begin molting later in summer. Juveniles only replace primaries 1 through 7 or 8, retaining the original outer two or three primaries. When these new primary feathers come in, they have smooth, round tips, often with a deeper color. Feathers not replaced are more narrow, ragged, and lighter in color. A bird with primaries 8, 9, or 10 showing a worn, ragged look is consequently a young of the year.

This works for virtually all game birds, as stated above, but another method is a bit more reliable for quail and doves. The outer several primary coverts are often edged with buff or pale color on juveniles, whereas the same feathers on adults are the uniform dark color of the primaries.

These aging methods are only mentioned briefly in the text facing each color plate, so refer back to here and the diagrams at the front if you are unsure. In no time at all, you'll be able to see these differences. A common difference among virtually all game birds that can be used only as a helper in identifying young and old is the overall appearance. Brighter, more vivid color is usually seen on adult birds; duller, paler color is seen on juveniles. Although subjective, this is a good start. The degree to which we can say an adult is truly an adult is only good through one year, meaning its second molting season. A pheasant with a 25-inch tail doesn't mean, for example, that it is five years old—it could be a second year bird with a long tail. So, for the purpose of this book, an adult is at least one year old.

Many upland birds have specific breeding displays that are fascinating to observe. Often these displays, which can be quite visual and vocal, occur in open areas where we can watch through binoculars, camera, or even with the naked eye. Some birds are monogamous (quail and doves), and others are polygamous (males and females breeding with more than one of the opposite sex, such as grouse, ptarmigans, pheasants, woodcock, etc.). Learning about and observing these displays adds much to the appreciation of these game birds.

RUFFED GROUSE *(Bonasa umbellus)*

Nicknames   Partridge, Pa'tridge, Ruff, Drummer

Average Size and Weight   17″ to 19″ — 1 to 1¾ lbs

Description

- The long, rounded tail of the ruffed grouse can be fanned out nearly 180 degrees, and each tailfeather is terminally barred with a black band followed by a gray tip. There are two basic color phases, gray and red, and this is most noticeable on the tail. Around the neck and upper back there is a black "ruff" of feathers, which is more prevalent in males.
- Sexes are similar, with a crest of head feathers and an overall brown and gray mottling above. The breast and sides are a creamy white, and the sides have brown bars extending through to the rump. Males typically exhibit a red/orange eye comb, unbroken terminal tailband, and two whitish dots on the rump feathers. Females typically have no eye comb, a broken terminal tailband, and one whitish dot on the rump feathers. The legs are feathered down to the base of the toes; in winter, both sexes (as with most grouse) develop firm protrusions off the toes for walking on snow (snowshoes).
- The outer two or three primaries are more rounded and smooth on adults than the more pointed and ragged primaries of juveniles.
- Ruffed grouse burst into flight with a loud and startling whirring of wings, reaching top speed in only several wingbeats. They disperse from family groups by midautumn.

Distribution / Habitat

- In the U.S., they are found throughout the northern Midwest (Minnesota east to Maine), south into parts of Virginia and Georgia, and western Montana to the West Coast; in Canada, they are found throughout most of the provinces and up into Alaska.
- Ruffed grouse prefer a mixture of deciduous trees and mixed woodlands, typically aspen and birch in successive stages from 10 to 40 years old, and some conifers. Other preferred vegetation includes dogwood, witch hazel, and alder.
- In winter, they prefer several inches to several feet of powdery snow for roosting purposes, diving down into a snow burrow for warmth and to avoid avian predators.

Food

- Insects, berries, leaves, buds, and seeds, with a high dependence on male catkins from aspen trees in winter.

Voice

- Rarely vocal.

Breeding

- In spring, males stake out territory on a log or rock from which they drum to attract females. They fan out their tails for support while beating their wings slowly at first, then rapidly. Air rushing through the wings makes a beating or drumming sound. After drumming, males often strut up and down the log with tails fanned out and ruff extended.

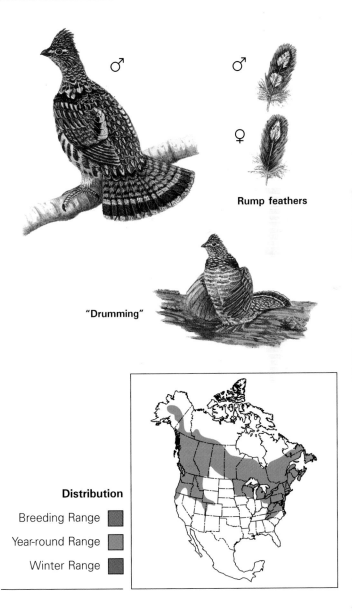

♂

♂

♀

Rump feathers

"Drumming"

Distribution

Breeding Range

Year-round Range

Winter Range

SPRUCE GROUSE *(Dendragapus canadensis)*

Nicknames   Fool hen, Canada grouse, Franklin's grouse

Average Size and Weight   15″ to 17″ — 1 to 1½ lbs

Description

- Males have gray to black upper parts, a black throat, and a black patch on the breast where the feathers are tipped heavily in white; eye combs are red, and white feathers border the black throat. Females have brown, black, and gray barring on the head, upper parts, and sides, with a yellow/gold tint, and mainly whitish underparts. They lack the male's black throat patch and breast patch tipped in white. Females are seen as either a red or gray phase.

- Both sexes have a black to dark brown unbarred tail with either a whitish or tawny terminal band at tip. Undertail coverts on each sex are gray/black with wide white tips.

- Juveniles can be distinguished from adults using the same methods as for ruffed grouse.

- When flushed or disturbed, spruce grouse usually fly to a branch of the nearest tree and observe the intruder, sometimes allowing one to walk within a very close distance. This tame behavior gave rise to their nickname, "fool hen."

Distribution / Habitat

- They are distributed throughout parts of the northern Great Lakes and eastern states, northern Rockies, Pacific Northwest, and most of Canada and Alaska. Habitat includes mixed coniferous forests and boreal forests, primarily balsam fir, spruce, and jack pine.

Food

- These grouse feed on some seeds, leaves, and berries, but their diet is comprised mainly of pine needles. Berries are eaten more in summer, but needles predominate for most of the year.

Voice

- Males typically make two different calls — one an aggressive series of calls and the other a single or series of low hoots during breeding season. Female calls range from high-pitched to low-pitched squeals and soft peeps and clucks.

Breeding

- The male stakes out breeding territory in a dense stand of trees, typically some species of pine. He does a basic strutting display with the tail held high and fanned so the predominately white undertail coverts are exposed. Wings are dropped and the neck is craned up, eye comb fully engorged, and neck feathers puffed out. The tail is also fanned from side to side, making a swishing sound as the feathers pass over each other. As a female approaches, the male might squat, rush her, bob his head, or flick his tail.

- Short aerial flights at different heights are also performed by males, mainly by spruce grouse found in the West. These flights sometimes end with two loud claps when the wings hit together on the backstroke.

♂

Black breast

♀

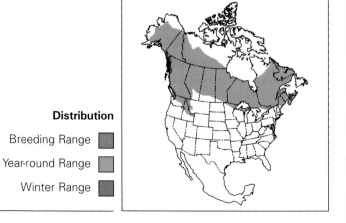

Distribution

Breeding Range

Year-round Range

Winter Range

BLUE GROUSE *(Dendragapus obscurus)*

Nicknames Sooty grouse, Richardson's grouse, Mountain grouse, Dusky grouse

Average Size and Weight 17″ to 23″ — 1¾ to 2¾ lbs

Description

- Blue grouse are bigger than the other woodland grouse. Males are mostly gray to slate blue on the head and upper parts, with mottled brown and black wings and back. Breast and underparts of male are vermiculated gray and white, without the black breast patch as in the spruce grouse. The undertail coverts are white, and leg feathers extend to the base of the middle toe. Males also have yellow/orange/red eye combs; the inflatable patch of skin on the neck during breeding display can be yellow to red to purple, with the bases of the feathers that move to expose the skin a bright white.

- Females are mottled brown, black, and gray over their entire body, and underparts are not white as in female spruce grouse. Barring on head is not present in males. Both sexes have similar dark brown to black tails, mostly not barred, and lighter to buff-colored tips. There are several subspecies of blue grouse, all very similar in appearance and separated by geographic location.

Distribution/Habitat

- Birds can be found in the Northwest to Pacific Northwest, south into Utah, Colorado, and California, and north into British Columbia and Alberta.

- Blue grouse prefer mixed woodlands (mainly aspen) and coniferous forests (mainly Douglas fir), mountain slopes, and shrubs. They move up mountain slopes as the year progresses, wintering toward the top in the conifers and moving down in the spring during breeding season. There are always some type of the above-mentioned trees in the area.

Food

- Primary food consists of Douglas fir needles. Other foods include berries, forbs, twigs, and seeds.

Voice

- Males might hoot during breeding season, and females sometimes utter low *cut-cut-cut* calls during flight.

Breeding

- Males strut with a fanned tail, enlarged eye combs, erect body, and engorged skin patches (gular sacs) on sides of neck. Wings are often drooped, and there is much head jerking, tail cocking, and hooting.

- Males also perform flight displays that vary from short flutters to jumps, sometimes involving a loud clap of the wings.

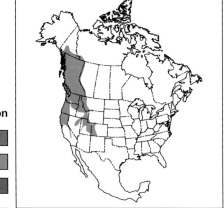

Distribution

Breeding Range

Year-round Range

Winter Range

SAGE GROUSE *(Centrocercus urophasianus)*

Nicknames   Sage hen, Sage cock, Sage chicken

Average Size and Weight   Males: 28″ to 31″ — 5 to 6½ lbs
Females: 20″ to 23″ — 2¾ to 3½ lbs

Description

- The largest of the North American grouse, the sage grouse is easy to identify by its size, the sagebrush habitat it is found in, its pointed tail, and black abdomen. Males can weigh twice as much as females. The male displays a large tail with pointed feathers during breeding. Its head is dark with fine plumes extending up and back, the throat is black, and breast feathers are white. These white breast feathers cover large yellow to greenish gular sacs that inflate during breeding display. Also during display, the yellow eye combs are engorged. The dark olive/yellow legs are feathered to the toe bases.

- Females resemble males except for the breeding display features, and their throats and breast are more barred than the male's black throat and white breast feathers. Their overall size, however, is about half that of the male.

- Immature sage grouse can be sexed in the same manner as the other grouse, using the outer two or three primaries (more pointed and rough or ragged, compared to round and smooth in adult).

Distribution / Habitat

- Sage grouse, as their name suggests, prefer sagebrush for their diet, as well as protection from predators and weather. Large spaces of rolling sage are needed to support populations of sage grouse. That is why they are found in the western mountain states, such as Montana, Wyoming, Colorado, Nevada, and Idaho.

Food

- Main diet is the buds, leaves, and shoots of sage. If snow covers this food during winter, they will move down to relatively low and flat elevations to find it. Other foods include grasses, forbs, berries, and insects.

Voice

- Both sexes utter certain types of high-pitched alarm calls, grunting, and fighting calls.

Breeding

- Male sage grouse gather on leks (dancing and courtship display areas) as soon as most of the snow is gone. No flying occurs in the courtship display, rather the display is confined to an involved strutting sequence. While the strutting sequence only lasts several seconds, it is comprised of many moves. Basically, it involves head and wing movement, with the long, pointed tailfeathers fanned; white breast feathers parting to expose the bare skin patches, which inflate and bulge outward, then collapse, resulting in two plopping noises.

Distribution

Breeding Range

Year-round Range

Winter Range

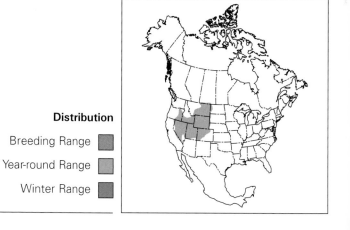

SHARP-TAILED GROUSE *(Tympanuchus phasianellus)*

Nicknames Sharptail, Prairie grouse, Sharpy

Average Size and Weight 16″ to 18″ — 1½ to 2½ lbs

Description

- Sharptails are so named for the tapered tail that appears to end in a point, although the two central tailfeathers are square at the tip. They are mottled brown, buff, and white. Sharptails are more white underneath and on the tail than prairie chickens. Markings on the breast are "V" shaped; wings are brown with ochre markings and white dots.

- To sex, examine the crown and tailfeathers. On the crown, where females have alternating dark brown and buff barring, males are more uniformly brown with light buff feather tips. On males, the central two tailfeathers are lighter with dark longitudinal markings on the entire length; the female's feathers are barred brown and buff the entire length of the rachis.

- Males exhibit enlarged yellow eye combs and purple air sacs during courtship display.

- Feet are feathered heavily to the base of the toes. Examine outer primaries for aging. When flushed, sharptails can fly great distances. By late fall and winter, flocks can number 100 or more.

Distribution/Habitat

- Sharptails inhabit the prairies and agricultural land of the Midwest and Western plains, and much of the Canadian provinces and Alaska. They prefer short prairie grass with a mixture of shrubbery in coulees and draws and cannot tolerate areas that are more than 50 percent hardwoods. For the easternmost populations on Michigan's Upper Peninsula, large tracts of brushy land are preserved or burned to control forestation.

Food

- Fruits, such as rose hips, and herbaceous plants, as well as goldenrod seeds, other forbs, catkins, buds, berries, and insects (especially grasshoppers in summer), and waste grain.

Voice

- Calls include cooing, *luk-a-luk* sounds, cackling, squeaking, and gobbling noises. Most vocalizations occur on the lek during courtship, but when flushed, a sound of *kuk-kuk-kuk-kuk-kuk* is often heard.

Breeding

- In spring, several to 20 or more males gather on leks to stake out prime central dancing territories to attract females. Flutter-jumping and cackling begins, then posturing as males square off against one another, heads lowered, wings drooped, purple air sacs enlarged, and tails erect. Males stomp their feet rapidly in place or move forward slightly while turning side to side, rapidly rattling the tailfeathers to produce a clicking noise. Males "dance" like this almost in harmony with one another, and it is quite a spectacle to see 15 males begin and end their displays together.

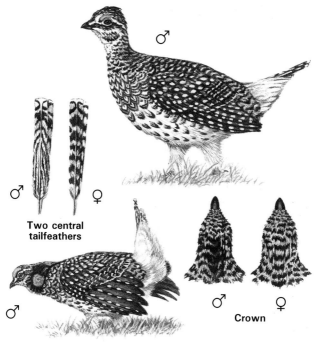

Two central
tailfeathers

Courtship display

Crown

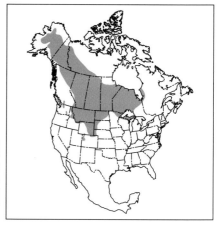

Distribution

Breeding Range

Year-round Range

Winter Range

GREATER PRAIRIE CHICKEN *(Tympanuchus cupido)*

Nicknames   Chicken, Pinnated grouse, Prairie grouse

Average Size and Weight   16″ to 19″ — 2 to 3 lbs

Description

- Greater prairie chickens are overall buff/white with dark brown barring over the entire body. On the necks are feathers called "pinnae," which are longer on males than females. These pinnae are pointed and can stick above the head like horns during display. The eye comb is yellow/orange, and the esophageal sacs are bright yellow and larger in males, paler and less noticeable in females. The dark, yellow/olive feet are feathered to the base of the toes. Aging is done by examining the primaries, as with the other grouse.

- Two methods to differentiate sexes involve examining tail and crown feathers. The tails of both sexes are short, dark brown/black and rounded, but the female's tail is heavily barred with white stripes, while the male's tail has little or no barring. Crown feathers of males are dark with light, buff edges, while females alternate dark and light bars.

- The lesser prairie chicken is found in very small numbers now in the U.S., and is smaller than the greater, with smaller pinnae and reddish/orange rather than yellow sacs on the neck.

Distribution /Habitat

- Chicken habitat is found on the tallgrass prairies of the Midwest and central plains. Kansas boasts the largest population of greater prairie chickens today, but other states, such as the Dakotas and Nebraska, have huntable populations.

Food

- Feed primarily on grains, such as corn, sorghum, oats, and wheat, grasses, soybeans, other similar vegetation, and insects. Where present, mast and buds are foraged. They fly into feeding fields once or twice per day in flocks of 10 to 25 or more.

Voice

- Besides several other cackling sounds, the main sound is a "booming" noise made during breeding display.

Breeding

- Booming is the collective term given to their courtship display. On the lek in spring, several to many males gather to boom and compete for the few females nearby. The tail is raised and pinnae erected above the lowered head. He then stamps his feet rapidly on the ground, often charging quickly at other males. The male performs three quick tail movements while making a quick three-note booming sound with air sacs engorging fully and then deflating. This process is repeated from first light to late morning, and the booming can be heard up to a half-mile or more. Jumping and cackling also occurs.

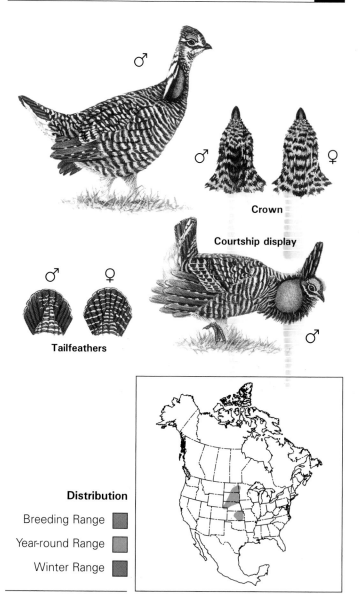

♂

Crown
♂ ♀

Courtship display

Tailfeathers
♂ ♀

♂

Distribution

Breeding Range

Year-round Range

Winter Range

WILLOW PTARMIGAN *(Lagopus lagopus)*

Nicknames Red grouse, Willow grouse, Alaskan ptarmigan

Average Size and Weight 15″ to 16″ — 1 to 1¾ lbs

Description

- Willow ptarmigan, like the other ptarmigan, can be differentiated from the other grouse species by the presence of feathering all the way to the tips of the toes in winter and by the upper tail coverts that extend to the tail tip and not the base.
- Ptarmigan go through a number of plumages to match habitat conditions. Willow ptarmigan have dark tails with white tips at all times, and males have red eye combs. In spring and summer, the brown feathers have a red tint and wings are white. In fall, males are more barred than rock ptarmigans; by winter, the white male lacks the black eye markings of the male rock ptarmigan. Females in spring and summer have heavier barring (not as rusty as the male) and, come fall, are more gray on top and whitish underneath. The winter female is entirely white except for the dark brown/black tail. The female lacks the red eye comb, and its tailfeathers are more brown compared to black in the male. The bill of the willow is thicker and appears heavier than the rock.
- Immature willows have a darker ninth primary compared to the eighth; on adults, it is quite similar on both feathers. The immature's eighth primary has considerably more gloss than the ninth and tenth primaries, where adults have similar amounts of gloss on these last three primaries.

Distribution/Habitat

- Willows are the most common ptarmigan in North America, ranging from all of northern Canada through most of Alaska.
- Habitat is mainly tundra or similar habitat on mountainsides or boreal forests. Low willow and birch shrubbery (up to 7 or 8 feet) on valley bottoms and foothills and along streams are preferred.

Food

- Main foods are buds and twigs of willow. Other foods consist of berries (blueberries, crowberries, etc.), insects, alder and birch twigs and buds, and various other leaves.

Voice

- Quite vocal, uttering calls during flight, breeding displays and flights, territorial disputes, and aggression, ranging from *cowba* to *crrro* to *go-back-go-back-go-back* calls and other similar sounds.

Breeding

- Both sexes participate in breeding displays. Males may face off or stand alongside one another, strutting with head, eye combs, and tail erect, wings drooped, and mouth open. Males might do several courtship displays, such as the song flight, or walk by a female while fanning its tail or around her with head high and undertail coverts exposed, run at her with head down and tail fanned, or bow to her continually with the body held low to the ground. Both sexes wag their heads.

Fall plumage

Winter   Spring   Summer

Tail black throughout year

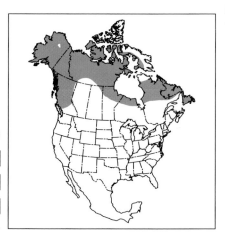

Distribution

Breeding Range

Year-round Range

Winter Range

ROCK PTARMIGAN *(Lagopus mutus)*

Nickname   Arctic grouse, Snow grouse

Average Size and Weight   12″ to 14″ — 1 to 1½ lbs

Description

- Rock ptarmigan, like the willow, have dark tails, which help distinguish them from white-tailed ptarmigan in all seasons. Males tend to be more finely marked with brown, black, and gray, lacking much of the overall chestnut appearance of the willow. Females tend to be more finely marked than female willows, with barring extending from the breast to the throat, but differentiating between the two females is extremely difficult. Rock ptarmigan go through similar plumage differences as the willow, but in winter, the male rock ptarmigan has a black eye stripe, which females usually lack. The bills of the rock are smaller and blacker than the willow's, but wings are white year-round, as are the willow's.
- Age rock ptarmigan using the same procedure as the willow ptarmigan.

Distribution / Habitat

- Rock ptarmigan range from the tundra regions throughout all of Canada and Alaska and into the Arctic. They can be found in willows or shrubbery and higher lichen-covered or rocky slopes above the timberline.

Food

- Buds, flowers, and catkins of dwarf birch and buds and twigs of willow, as well as a variety of plants (horsetail), berries, and seeds in the spring and summer.

Voice

- Loud territorial and courtship calls resound in the form of *ka-ka-ka-ka-ka*, along with a variety of similar sounds.

Breeding

- Rock ptarmigan defend large territories with long aerial display flights or aggression and fighting, sometimes resulting in the death of the loser. To attract a female or defend territory, the male performs a song flight. This involves a flight as high as 200 feet or more, cackling at the beginning, until he sets his wings at the top and begins to sail downward with set wings and fanned tail, cackling again, until landing with tail erect and wings dragging on the ground. The entire time, the eye combs become quite red and engorged. He may rush or bow to a nearby female.

♂

♀

♂

Winter

Tail black throughout year

Distribution

Breeding Range

Year-round Range

Winter Range

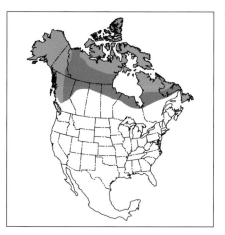

WHITE-TAILED PTARMIGAN *(Lagopus leucurus)*

Nicknames   Snow grouse

Average Size and Weight   12″ to 14″ — ¾ to 1 lb

Description

- White-tailed ptarmigan are easily distinguished from both rock and willow ptarmigan by a white tail rather than a dark brown or black tail. Females tend to be more heavily barred and yellowish; males have fine vermiculations. Males during the summer have white wings, belly, undertail coverts and tail. Females also display the red eye comb, a difference from the other two ptarmigan. In winter, both sexes are virtually identical.

- Aging white-tailed ptarmigan is done by looking at the outer two primaries and primary coverts for any dark pigment—if present, then it is probably an immature bird.

Distribution / Habitat

- Their range is far less than that of the other two ptarmigan and extends from portions of Alaska down through the Pacific Northwest and into areas of the Rocky Mountains. They prefer alpine willows and tundra above the timberline.

Food

- Diet consists primarily of alder, willow, and birch catkins, and a variety of leaves, seeds, and flowers.

Voice

- Very vocal, especially during breeding season. It has many calls, but the underlying tone is a *cuk-cuk-cuk-caaak* or other various clucking or guttural screams.

Breeding

- Males perform territorial flights like the willow and rock, called scream flights, where the bird makes low, four-syllable calls spaced apart several seconds while rising and gliding. While on the ground, similar sounds are made, along with flattening out and running or strutting upright and still, eye combs engorged. With a female, the male performs various head bowing, pecking, and circling techniques, with tail fanned and head tilted so she can see the red eye combs.

♂

♀

♂

Winter

Tail white throughout year

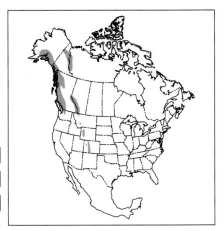

Distribution

Breeding Range

Year-round Range

Winter Range

CHUKAR *(Alectoris chukar)*

Nickname Red-legged partridge, Rock partridge

Average Size and Weight 13″ — 1 to 1¾ lbs

Description

- The chukar is a beautiful import from Europe. It has a gray breast, crown, and back, creamy underparts, white sides with black bars, buff or white face with black eye stripe extending down to form a black necklace, and red bill, eye ring, and legs. No bird closely resembles it in North America.
- Sexes are too identical to tell, even with measurements; however, some feel that males may have brighter, stockier beaks and feet, but you'll need two to several in hand to make any kind of comparison. Juveniles tend to be smaller, with a more mottled or muted appearance.
- These birds move in coveys of 5 or 6 to as many as 30 or 40.

Distribution/Habitat

- Chukars inhabit rugged areas west of the Rockies to the West Coast and up into parts of British Columbia. They prefer rocky or semirocky slopes of mountains or canyons, with a mixture of sagebrush and other grasses. The climate is quite arid, although a stream or river is often nearby.

Food

- Diet consists of a variety of seeds and grasses, mainly the seeds of cheatgrass, Russian thistle, and downy chess. Other foods can include alfalfa leaves, clover leaves, fruits, berries, and insects, such as grasshoppers.

Voice

- Vocal birds, they utter sounds like *chuk-chuk-chukara* or *chuk-chuk-chuk-chuk*, making them easy to pinpoint (but not necessarily easy to pursue). They also utter higher-pitched alarm calls.

Breeding

- The *chuk-chuk-chuka* calls can deter other males during breeding season. When a female approaches, the male struts, cocks his head, and circles her slowly, eventually leading to copulation.

Distribution

Breeding Range

Year-round Range

Winter Range

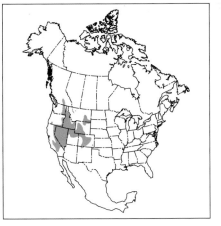

GRAY PARTRIDGE *(Perdix perdix)*

Nicknames   Hungarian partridge, Hun

Average Size and Weight   13″ — ½ to 1 lb

Description

- The Hun, as it is most often referred to, is a plump, gray and brown bird. The sexes are nearly identical, with a tan face mask and throat, gray crown, and black and cream vermiculations on the gray neck and breast. The sides have similar vermiculations but are barred with rusty bands, and the tail is a rust color. The back is gray and brown, with rusty vermiculations, and the shoulders are brown with yellow/buff streaking. On both sexes, the belly is white/cream, but on males, there is a pronounced rusty horseshoe pattern. Females are overall paler, but that can be quite subjective, especially early in the season.
- Sexing is simple once in hand by observing scapular feathers. Males have a thin, longitudinal yellow/buff stripe running down the rachis. This stripe is thicker in females, and they also have two to four horizontal buff crossbars on these feathers.
- Aging is similar to that of the grouse: observing if the outer two primaries are more pointed and frayed (immatures) or more rounded and smooth (adults).
- Huns are a covey bird consisting of 10 to 15 or more individuals.

Distribution /Habitat

- The Hun is a bird of the open. It is commonly found in prairie grasslands and around agricultural fields, primarily wheat fields, of the northern Midwestern states and southcentral Canadian provinces. Often it can be found around old, brushy, abandoned homesteads bordered by agricultural fields. It also prefers brushy canyons or coulees, or steeper, semirocky slopes.

Food

- Primary foods are grains, such as wheat, corn, and barley; seeds of some grasses, including foxtail, crabgrass, and others; grasses of alfalfa, clover, and wild mustard. A host of insects, when available, are also eaten.

Voice

- Not very vocal, Huns utter *kee-ak* calls during breeding season, and when flushed, make alarm calls in a squeaking fashion that resembles an old rusty gate opening.

Breeding

- Males strut in circles uttering the *kee-ak* sound once a female is near.

♂

♂

♀

Scapular feathers

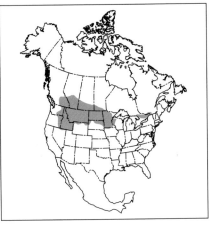

Distribution

Breeding Range

Year-round Range

Winter Range

RING-NECKED PHEASANT *(Phasianus colchicus)*

Nicknames   Ringneck, Rooster, Cock

Average Size and Weight   Males: 31″ to 35″ — 2¼ to 3 lbs
                                  Females: 21″ to 24″ — 1¾ to 2¼ lbs

Description

- The ringneck is North America's most popular imported game bird. Males (roosters) are easy to distinguish from the much paler and mottled brown color of the hen. Its tail is long and pointed, with horizontal black barring; a multicolored body of bronze, yellow, and orange feathers with black markings on each; and a blue/green rump. The wings are overall light to silver in color. The head is an iridescent green and violet, with black ear tufts, red wattle and eye, and distinguishing white ring around most of the neck. Males also have spurs of varying length on their legs, and females do not. The female's tail is much shorter than the male's. (The more woodland Sichuan species lacks the white ring and is not abundant in North America.)

- Holding the bird by the lower mandible is a good indicator of an adult if it does not collapse—it will collapse under the weight of the bird in juveniles. Juveniles have light gray spurs that are more rounded than the black, more pointed spurs of adult birds.

Distribution / Habitat

- Ringnecks inhabit much of the farmland, prairie grassland, brushy hedgerows, creek and river bottoms, and woodland edges of the northern United States and southern Canada. Birds can be found from coast to coast, with the bulk of the populations centering in the nation's central Midwest. Ringnecks have responded to management practices such as the Conservation Reserve Program (CRP) and flourish as they once did years ago.

Food

- Grains such as corn, wheat, barley, milo, sorghum, oats, and others. They also eat seeds and leaves of other grasses and insects. They often leave their roost early to midmorning and fly or walk to feeding areas, returning late in the day to feed again before going back to the roost.

Voice

- Main call is a *caw-cack*, with an emphasis on the first syllable. A rooster often sounds off a series of these calls when flushed.

Breeding

- During spring, the audible crowing of the rooster can be heard in the morning and evening. The male crows to attract females and ward off rival males. Following a crow, the male flaps his wings loudly, wattle fully engorged, and struts. Rival males fight vigorously, using sharp spurs, beaks, and wings. Near a female, a rooster puffs out his feathers and leans to the side toward her, fanning his tailfeathers.

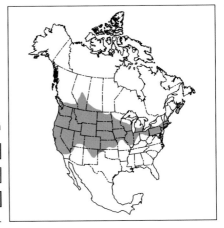

Distribution

Breeding Range

Year-round Range

Winter Range

AMERICAN WOODCOCK *(Scolopax minor)*

Nicknames   Timberdoodle, Woody, Bog snipe

Average Size and Weight   10″ to 12″ — 5 to 8 ounces
Females are at the extreme end of these measurements

Description

- Members of the shorebird family, woodcock thrive in the uplands, migrating north and south throughout their range. They are solitary and fly alone, not in flocks.
- They are round/oval, stout, and camouflaged in light and dark brown, rust, and black. The long and flexible bill aids in retrieving earthworms and grubs deep in the mud. Large eyes are set high and far back on the head; crown is thickly barred in black; and breast and belly are light tan. Tailfeathers are black and white (luminescent in low light).
- Sexes are nearly identical, but males overall are smaller, and total body mass and bill length should be examined. The outer three primary feathers also indicate sex, being relatively the same size on females and extremely narrow on males.
- Aging is done by observing the light terminal and dark subterminal bands at the tips of the inner secondary feathers. These feathers are mottled and blurry on adults, and the bands are distinct on juveniles.
- When flushed, woodcock often angle upward toward the leaf canopy, dodging limbs and appearing to fly faster than they really are. Wind moving through the outer primaries creates a twittering sound.

Distribution / Habitat

- They are found in all states east of the Mississippi, but heaviest concentrations are found in the northern states, New England, and southeastern Canada. They winter in most of the southern Gulf States, where ground rarely freezes and food is available. During migration, woodcock follow stream and river courses.
- They are found in moist woodlands, tag alder thickets, near clearings and field edges, and clearcuts of aspen from 5 to 15 years old, often with bracken fern.

Food

- They feed almost exclusively on earthworms but also eat grubs, sow bugs, larvae, and other insects. Crepuscular, they feed and are most active just before dawn and just after dusk, flying to and from loafing sites.

Voice

- Vocal mainly during breeding season when males utter low *peents* and melodious warbles and chirping.

Breeding

- Males perform sky dance courtship flights after establishing territory and make penetrating, nasal *peents* (a soft warble precedes each *peent*). Flight is a long, circular path upward, and the male begins a melodious series of warbling and chirping at the top, finally sailing back to the same displaying area. *Peenting* and flights are repeated throughout the evening. A number of males can occupy the same dancing area.

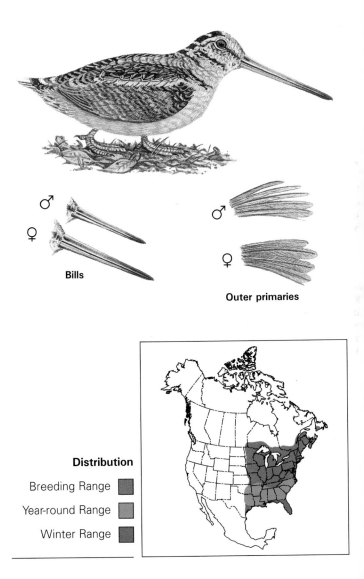

Bills

Outer primaries

Distribution

Breeding Range

Year-round Range

Winter Range

COMMON SNIPE *(Gallinago gallinago)*

Nicknames — Jacksnipe, Wilson's snipe

Average Size and Weight — 10″ to 12″ — 3¼ to 6 ounces

Description

- Common snipe are more slender than woodcock, mottled dark brown, black, and tan on their chest and back. The dark mottling on the upper chest can appear as streaking. The head is buff with dark stripes on the crown and through the eye; the breast and belly are white, and sides are white with short, horizontal bars. The bill is long and slender, as are the yellow/gray feet. The tail is rusty with white tip and black barring.

- Sexes are too similar to accurately distinguish, and by midautumn, aging is as difficult to determine.

- They can be easily identified by a relatively thunderous flush and the ensuing zigzag flight pattern, often ending with a near-vertical dive to the landing. Be careful, however; snipe can be found in the same type of habitat as other, protected shorebirds. Snipe most often flush singly, whereas other shorebirds usually flush in groups of 2 or 3 to 5 or 10.

Distribution /Habitat

- Snipe are found coast to coast, especially in the northern United States and most of Canada. They migrate to most of the southern states.

- They prefer shallow, wet areas in fields or floodings where they can wade or hop around on clumps of grass. Bogs, marshes, and river and stream edges are prime habitat for snipe.

Food

- Similar food as woodcock, using the same techniques when probing for worms and grubs, except snipe are more likely to probe in shallow water. Insects, such as mosquitoes, flies, beetles, and a host of other food, from nymphs and dragonflies to mollusks and spiders to grass seeds, are all part of the diet.

Voice

- The two main sounds common snipe make are the loud *scape!* call when flushed, and the winnowing sound made during courtship flights. The *scape!* call distinguishes the snipe from other shorebirds, which most often peep when taking flight.

Breeding

- Males perform aerial territorial and courtship flights, called winnowing, during the spring breeding season, flying as high as 200 to 350 feet and diving at speeds up to 50 mph. This speed provides sufficient wind through the last two rigid tailfeathers to vibrate them, causing a *who-who-who-who* sound that can be heard up to a half mile away or more. Flights take place in early morning or at dusk.

Distribution

Breeding Range

Year-round Range

Winter Range

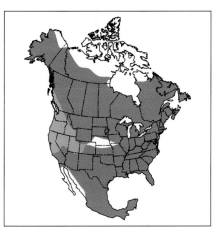

NORTHERN BOBWHITE QUAIL *(Colinus virginianus)*

Nicknames   Bobwhite

Average Size and Weight   9″ to 10″ — 5 to 8 ounces

Description

- Bobwhites are the most common of the six species of quail in North America and were so named for their call, *bob-White!* Sexes are easy to distinguish by plumage. Males have a rust/brown crown and dark brown/black stripe on cheek and white stripe from bill to back of nape, and white throat with black necklace. On females, the dark markings of the male are brown, and the white mask of the male are yellow/buff. Their plump body is rust and brown, with rust streaking on the sides and a darker brown and gray back. The belly is white with black "V" markings, and gray tail.

- To age, look at the outer two or three primary coverts. Juveniles have pale buff-tipped edges, whereas on the adult, they are the uniform gray/brown of the primaries.

- Bobwhites, as with all quail, are covey birds, and average 10 to 20 or more birds in a covey. They flush together or staggered, with a loud buzzing sound similar to large bees, heading different directions for flights of 75 to 150 yards.

Distribution / Habitat

- Bobwhites live in farmland, pastureland, and rolling agricultural land where there is an abundance of thick fencerows or brushy edges. A brushy treeline on the edge of a cropped field, roadside, or CRP field is prime habitat in the Midwest. Bobwhites in the South — Georgia, Mississippi, northern Florida, etc. — prefer tall, open pine woods with brushy understory, and those in the Southwest can be found on arid slopes or brushy canyons with a water source nearby. They do not hold up well in cold, harsh winter conditions. The best numbers are located in Kansas, Missouri, Oklahoma, Texas, Georgia, Alabama, and Mexico.

Food

- Seeds of grasses and legumes, berries (blackberries, raspberries, rose hips, etc.), peanuts, leaves of clover and other plants, and grains, such as wheat, milo, sorghum, rye, and corn; they also eat insects.

Voice

- Main call is the *bob-bob White!*, or *bob White!*, with the emphasis on *white*!, and sounding as if whistled.

Breeding

- The male calls repeatedly to announce territory and attract a mate. Once a female approaches, he bows his head and spreads his wings, strutting around her while showing off his white head markings. Call is very audible on quiet spring mornings.

Distribution

Breeding Range

Year-round Range

Winter Range

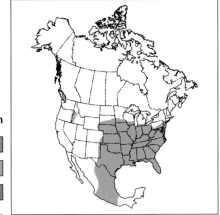

MONTEZUMA (MEARNS') QUAIL
(Cyrtonyx montezumae)

Nicknames Harlequin quail, Painted quail

Average Size and Weight 8″ to 10″ — 4 to 7 ounces

Description

- Mearns' is the common subspecies of Montezuma quail in the U.S. and northern Mexico. Males have the characteristic black head with intricate white face mask; the crown is mottled on top, and a large, rusty brown patch at the rear protrudes back over the neck. The sides are black with white spots, and a deep cinnamon/brown band runs from neck to belly. The tail is stubby and the undertail and belly black.

- Females are light brown on the face with a less distinct pattern and light brown or pink overall. Markings on back are similar to male's. Nails on feet are extra long and aid in digging and scratching leaves and dirt for bulbs and tubers.

- The outer two or three primary coverts have buff edging or barring on juveniles and distinct white spots or barring on adults.

- Coveys range from 10 to 12 birds early in the season to 3 to 8 later on. Family groups make up each covey—both adults and the clutch; there is no recruitment if covey numbers drop. Their first defense is to remain motionless even when danger is only a few feet away. They are perfectly camouflaged for their terrain. Coveys flush in staggered twos and threes.

- Coveys typically roost on a roughly barren, southwest-facing slope, a place where the last sun might have been warming the ground.

Distribution/Habitat

- The well-adapted Mearns' quail lives in the harsh climate of the arid, rocky Southwest. Prefers bottomlands and slopes of canyons where there is an abundance of emery oak and Arizona white oak, which offer shade for coolness and mast for food; a moderate amount of grass aids in concealment. These birds respond well during years of good precipitation in July and August, and it is believed that over-grazing and hunting do not significantly impact their populations because much of their range is inaccessible to cattle and people.

- Best populations exist in southwestern Arizona, southeastern New Mexico, and Mexico.

Food

- Scratches and roots with its thick beak for bulbs, roots, and tubers of plants, such as chulfa and nut grass; also eats acorns, legumes, grass seeds, fruits, and insects. Moisture is taken from food.

Voice

- Quiet; main call is a series of soft, trailing whistles.

Breeding

- Little is known about their breeding displays, except that they are monogamous like the other quail.

Long nails

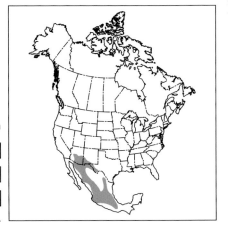

Distribution

Breeding Range

Year-round Range

Winter Range

SCALED QUAIL *(Callipepla squamata)*

Nicknames   Scalie, Blue quail, Cottontop

Average Size and Weight   10″ to 11″ — 6¼ to 7½ ounces

Description

- Scaled quail are an overall gray/blue bird with a high, distinct crest tipped in white. Their backs and rump are duller gray. The feathers on the bluer upper back, neck, and lighter blue/gray chest, breast, and belly are edged in black, giving them the appearance of scales.

- Sexes are difficult to distinguish, but males tend to have a more uniformly gray face with brown ear patch, while the female's face appears to be streaked with gray. Males also tend to have buff/cream throats and females tend to have light streaking on their throats. The male's crest can be a bit longer and/or whiter on top, but this is all very subjective. Juveniles can be determined using the same method as the bobwhite—checking the pale tips on the outer primary coverts.

- Coveys consist of 20 to 30 birds, but in winter can number as high as 100 to 150 or more. Scalies prefer to run rather than fly when danger is near, making them a tough game bird to hunt. The singles hold tighter once flushed, but getting them to flush at all can be tricky.

Distribution /Habitat

- Scalies be found in portions of Arizona, New Mexico, Texas, Colorado, Kansas, Oklahoma, and Mexico.

- Another desert quail, these hardy birds prefer mesas, plateaus, and river valleys of dry, barren grassland with intermixed sagebrush, mesquite, cactuses, and other shrubbery. Often seek shelter in yucca or some variety of cacti. Coveys make daily trips to water.

Food

- Seeds of grasses, mesquite, ragweed, and sunflower, as well as grains, including corn and sorghum. They also eat a host of insects.

Voice

- Location call is a long, whistling *pea-KOS!* Males may utter loud *wock* calls.

Breeding

- Males call from perches to attract a female and to announce territory.

Distribution

Breeding Range

Year-round Range

Winter Range

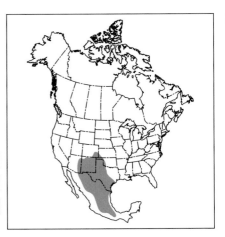

GAMBEL'S QUAIL *(Callipepla gambelii)*

Nicknames   Arizona quail, Desert quail

Average Size and Weight   10″ to 11″ — 5¾ to 7½ ounces

Description

- Gambel's quail is commonly confused with valley quail because of the similar colors and topknot plume on top of the head, but a few key characteristics make identification easy. The male has a rusty crown with black forehead and throat, and a white stripe runs above the eye and encircles the black throat. A distinctive black plume extends forward out from the forehead in a crescent shape. The breast and upper neck are gray/blue, and the upper neck and nape feathers are edged in black. The back is olive/brown and sides are rust with white marks. A cream patch is on the lower breast and black patch is on the belly. No scaling is present on the belly as there is in the valley quail.

- Female Gambel's are more drab than the male, with a dull, brown-streaked head and black topknot, similar body coloring, but no black belly patch.

- Use the same method of the primary coverts as with the bobwhite for aging. Also observe the outer two primaries—they are more pointed and frayed in juveniles and rounded and smooth in adults.

- Native to Arizona, Gambel's are its most popular game bird. Coveys range from 12 to 25 and up to 50 or more birds. They run rather than fly, but not as much as scaled quail.

Distribution / Habitat

- They are found in the Southwest, primarily Arizona, New Mexico, California, and Texas, and Mexico.

- Prime Gambel's habitat consists of river bottoms or washes lined with thick growths of mesquite, typically under 5000 feet elevation. Grassy understory with room to move is important. Inhabits thick, thorny shrubbery or willows along streams or creeks or some permanent water source. Other vegetation to look for is hackberry, catclaw, saguaro, prickly pear, burroweed, snakeweed, brittlebush, and more.

Food

- Seeds of mesquite and other grasses; also leaves and grains, insects, berries, and fruits of various cacti, like prickly pear.

Voice

- Main call is a *chi-CA-go-go*, sounded especially after a covey scatters. They also utter *wit-wit-wit* calls among themselves when in the covey.

Breeding

- Male perches and calls out audible *caw* calls in spring to attract a lost mate or a new one.

Cream-colored belly without "scales"

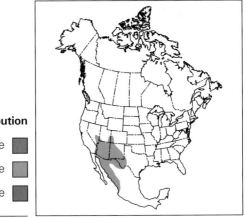

Distribution

Breeding Range

Year-round Range

Winter Range

VALLEY QUAIL *(Callipepla californicus)*

Nicknames California quail, Blue quail

Average Size and Weight 10″ to 11″ — 5 to 6½ ounces

Description

- Often called California quail, valley quail is the correct common name. This bird is often confused with the Gambel's quail because of the similar coloration and dark topknot plume. Males have similar coloration on the head to the Gambel's, including protruding teardrop plume, but the valley's forehead is brown, not black. The sides are more brown than rust, with white streaks, and the back is a brown/olive color. The pale blue/gray breast leads into buff belly feathers tipped with black, giving it the characteristic scaling appearance similar to scaled quail but different than the Gambel's. The combination of the topknot and scaling identify it as a valley quail.
- The female is similar in the body but lacks the black, white, and rust on the head of the male, and its plume is smaller.
- Aging is done using the same methods as with the Gambel's quail.
- Typical coveys of 30 to 50 birds are common, and in winter, coveys can be as large as 100 to 200 or more; and they run like bandits.

Distribution / Habitat

- Valley quail inhabit valleys, foothills, scrubby grassland, farms, suburbs, ranches, and woodlands with openings, allowing access to a nearby water source, such as a stream or river. They are mostly found along the West Coast.

Food

- They feed regularly in the morning and evening on grasses, buds, clover seeds, acorns, berries, and insects. Gambel's quail walk to and from feeding areas and rest and drink at watering holes in large numbers.

Voice

- Assembly call of the valley quail when scattered is a *ca-RO-bo*.

Breeding

- Unmated males perch and make *caw* calls to attract a mate.

♂

♀

Belly "scaled" on both sexes

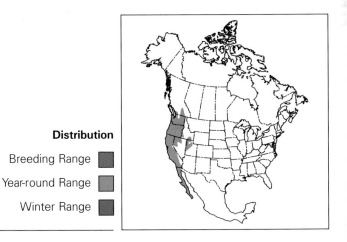

Distribution

Breeding Range

Year-round Range

Winter Range

MOUNTAIN QUAIL *(Oreortyx pictus)*

Nicknames   Plumed quail, Mountain partridge

Average Size and Weight   11″ to 12″ — 8 to 10¼ ounces

Description

- The mountain quail is the largest North American quail and is easy to identify by its two long, thin, straight head plumes. Sexes are nearly identical, although these plumes are shorter among females. They have a blue/gray head, neck, and breast. The chestnut/red chin and throat is lined on each side with white. The belly and sides are a deep chestnut/red with white bands and thinner black tips. The back and wings are olive/brown, and this color extends up a bit farther into the neck on the female; however, it is quite subjective.
- Aging is done by the same method as the bobwhite.
- Coveys consist anywhere from 3 or 4 to 15 to 20 birds. They nest at elevations of 10,000 feet but move down as the season progresses; prefer running rather than flying to evade danger.

Distribution / Habitat

- This species can be found in the mountain regions of the West Coast, including Oregon, Washington, Idaho, and California.
- Mountain quail live in thick, brushy areas of mountains, mountain meadows, and along edges of conifer stands. At lower elevations during the summer and fall, they prefer scrubby grasslands and thick, brushy areas near water.

Food

- Clover, legumes, bulbs, seeds of sumac, pines, sweet clover, hawthorn, and berries and fruits (serviceberry, grapes, snowberry, hackberry), as well as a variety of insects.

Voice

- Two main calls are *plu-ark* and a softly whistled *wh-wh-wh*.

Breeding

- Male whistles the *plu-ark* call from a perch to attract a mate. Like other quail, they are monogamous.

Two thin, straight plumes

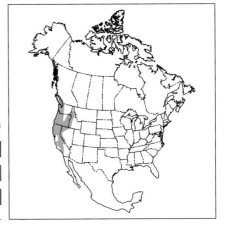

Distribution

Breeding Range

Year-round Range

Winter Range

MOURNING DOVE *(Zenaida macroura)*

Nicknames   Turtle dove

Average Size and Weight   12″ — 3 to 5 ounces

Description

- The mourning dove is the most widely distributed and popular game bird in the United States, even though there are still a number of states where they are not a legal game bird. It is a petite bird with an overall gray/brown back and light brown head, chest, and breast. The bill is thin and eye ring light blue. Often there are tinges of pink or yellow on the throat and neck of the male. Black marks are found on the cheek and wings; thin, pointed tailfeathers are tipped in white. The legs and feet are red.
- Flight is swift and wings make a whistling sound.
- Sexes of adults can be distinguished by the iridescent, colorful pattern on the sides of the neck that persist in the male but are absent in the female. In juveniles, sexing can only be reliably done by internal examination. On the wings of juvenile doves, the primary coverts are buff-tipped, and the ninth and tenth primaries are edged in white. Adults have uniformly gray primary coverts and primaries.

Distribution/Habitat

- Mourning doves prefer open areas, such as farmland, hedgerows, woodland edges, and agricultural fields. They are often seen perched in trees or power lines around and in urban areas. They have adapted widely across the nation, from the agricultural fields of southern Canada to the arid desert conditions of the southwestern states and coast to coast.
- Mourning doves typically water in large flocks at watering holes, ponds, or stock tanks in the evening before roosting.

Food

- They feed almost exclusively on the seeds of several grasses, including foxtail and yellow wood sorrel. They also eat waste grain—corn, wheat, oats, milo, rye, etc.

Voice

- Mournful call of the mourning dove is a four-note call of *coooah-coo-coo-coo*, with the first *coo* low and an emphasis on *ah*, then three lower, similar *coos*.

Breeding

- The mourning dove has the longest breeding season of any other game bird, from April through September. Calling is the main territorial defense as well as the male's way of attracting a female. When a female approaches, the male continues to call while waltzing around her. It is believed that they mate for life.

Tail pointed

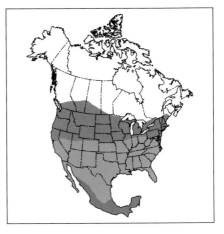

Distribution

Breeding Range

Year-round Range

Winter Range

WHITE-WINGED DOVE *(Zenaida asiatica)*

Nicknames Whitewing

Average Size and Weight 11″ — 4 to 5 ounces

Description

- Whitewings are a bit stockier than the mourning dove and tend to fly with a little less enthusiasm than their counterpart. The white patch on the leading edges of the wings gives them their name, and large white tips are also present on the shorter, more rounded tailfeathers. They are gray/brown overall, more gray than the mourning dove, with a wide, dark blue eye ring and a black spot that sits on the lower cheek. The bill is longer than a mourning dove's, and the legs and feet are red. Whitewings also lack the black spots on the upper wings of the mourning dove.

- Sexes are nearly identical; however, the slightly larger males tend to have a purple/red nape and yellow/green sheen on their necks. Aging is difficult, but juveniles tend to have buff-tipped primary coverts and primaries.

Distribution / Habitat

- White-winged doves are a bird of the dry Southwest and Mexico, which makes identification of a dove in most other parts of the country easy. They prefer heavily-branched areas of mesquite and saltcedar, open rangelands, and fruit groves. They roost and feed in large groups like the mourning dove. Primarily a bird of Mexico, U.S. populations are found in areas of southern California, Arizona, New Mexico, and Texas.

Food

- Seeds of sunflowers, doveweed, other native trees and shrubs, grasses, and legumes. They also feed on fruits of several cactuses, such as saguaro, and other fruits.

Voice and Breeding

- Males sound hollow territory calls of *kook-koo* while performing a long, arced, gliding display flight. Males also make a *two-boots-for-you* call, much like a barred owl, except softer, during courtship and territorial displays.

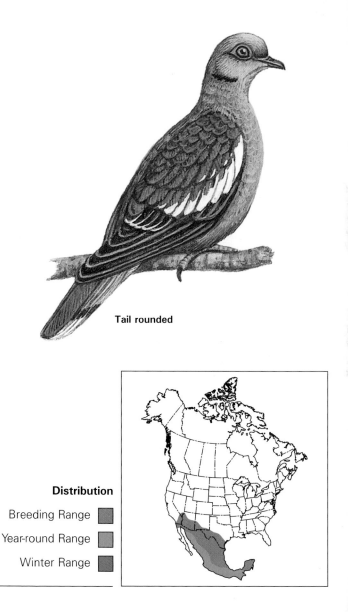

Tail rounded

Distribution

Breeding Range

Year-round Range

Winter Range

WILD TURKEY *(Meleagris gallopavo)*

Nicknames   Gobbler, Tom (males)

Average Size and Weight   Males: 27″ to 49″ — 16 to 25 lbs
Females: 27″ to 49″ — 9 to 13 lbs

Description

- The wild turkey is the largest North American game bird and one of the easiest to identify. The head is bare of feathers and consists of fleshy carnucles of gray/pink (females) or blue and red (males). The fleshy "snood" extends over the beak from the forehead of the male (very small in females). Body feathers are varying shades of bronze and black, with black barring, and exhibit an overall sheen from bronze to green. Black wings are barred with white, and the black tail is heavily barred with different shades of brown or buff, with a thick black subterminal band and brown to buff or white terminal band. The long legs and strong feet are scarlet/red in color, and males sport spurs that can be a half-inch to an inch or longer, especially on older birds. Males also have a noticeable beard, a hair-like extension from the breast that ranges from 2 to 10 inches or more. Some females may have a small beard. A female is called a "jenny," and a young turkey is called a "poult."

- Sexing is quite easy—males tend to have a brighter head of blue and red (especially in the spring breeding season), a noticeable beard, and are bigger overall. Females do not have spurs and typically no beard.

- Aging can be done by one of several methods. One is to look at beard length—the shorter the beard, the more likely it is to be a "jake" or juvenile male; the longer it is, the more likely it will be at least in its second season. If the central tailfeathers extend beyond the tips of the others, it most likely will be a juvenile, whereas an adult is uniformly tipped. And last, the spur length is a good indicator of older or younger birds—much the same as beard length but more reliable.

- Turkeys prefer running to evade danger and can do so with a great burst of speed; however, they are strong flyers for short distances. They roost in trees, often the same tree or area, and separate by sexes, flying down in the morning to gather. They move in flocks of 10 to 30 or 40, and winter flocks can be as high as 80 or more birds.

- The five subspecies we are concerned with that live in North America are the Eastern, Merriam's, Rio Grande, Florida, and Gould's. They are slightly morphologically different and more geographically different. For the most part, the visual differences are subtle, but as a basis for identification, look at the upper tail coverts and tail tips for differences in coloration. These feathers are chocolate brown on the Eastern and Florida turkeys, buff to white color on the Merriam's, yellowish on the Rio Grande's, and appear white on the Gould's. The white bars of the primary wing feathers of the Florida subspecies are quite narrow, making the wing appear darker than the other subspecies. These bars tend to be wider in the other birds.

Eastern Wild Turkey

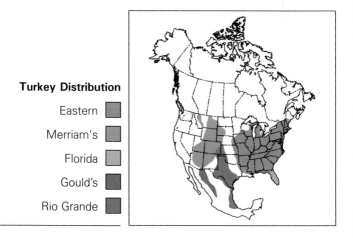

Turkey Distribution

Eastern

Merriam's

Florida

Gould's

Rio Grande

Distribution / Habitat

- Turkeys, no matter where they are in the country, prefer areas with trees for roosting. In the East, birds live in large woodland areas with a hardwood/deciduous mix. Pine, oak, and cypress forests in the west and south are preferred. All the subspecies prefer river bottoms, or areas where trees are usually located. Open areas, fields, or agricultural land should be nearby for feeding and scratching.
- Turkeys have made major comebacks in many parts of the U.S. Heaviest concentrations are east of the Mississippi, but all parts of the U.S. have birds. Knowing the geographic distribution of the wild turkey is the best method for identification. Some states, such as Washington, have successfully introduced three subspecies, so the subtleties of identification can be important in distinguishing each subspecies.

Food

- Turkeys scratch ground and leaves to reveal acorns, seeds, and nuts, and eat a host of other foods, including grains, grasses, berries, buds, insects, and even lizards, frogs, and other small animals.

Voice

- Turkeys are quite vocal, especially during breeding season. Females make a wide variety of calls, with the main sound a hoarse or raspy, audible *yelp*, or series of *yelps*. They also *put, cluck, cut, purr,* and *kee-kee*. Males make several of the *puts* and softer noises but are noted for their loud, resounding *gobbles*.

Breeding

- A common sight in the spring, flocks of turkeys can be seen in fields or woodland edges, with males displaying the familiar puffed body, fanned tail, and drooping wings. The male begins *gobbling* on the roost in the morning to let nearby hens know his location. Shortly after, he flies down and begins to strut and *gobble*, enticing one or many hens to visit. Fighting often breaks out between rival toms or a tom and a smaller jake. Mature gobblers strut around a female, tossing their tail side to side, and emitting low sounds called *drumming* and *spitting* while wagging their wingtips, often wearing them down several inches. Hunters imitate the call of the hen to entice a gobbler to pay them a visit—but since turkeys see and hear better than deer, any gobbler bagged is a trophy indeed.

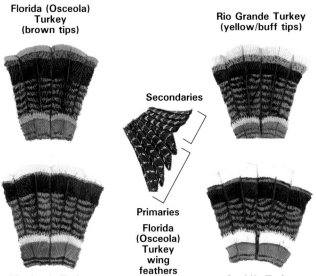

Florida (Osceola)
Turkey
(brown tips)

Rio Grande Turkey
(yellow/buff tips)

Secondaries

Primaries

Florida
(Osceola)
Turkey
wing
feathers

Merriam's Turkey
(light buff tips)

Gould's Turkey
(white tips)

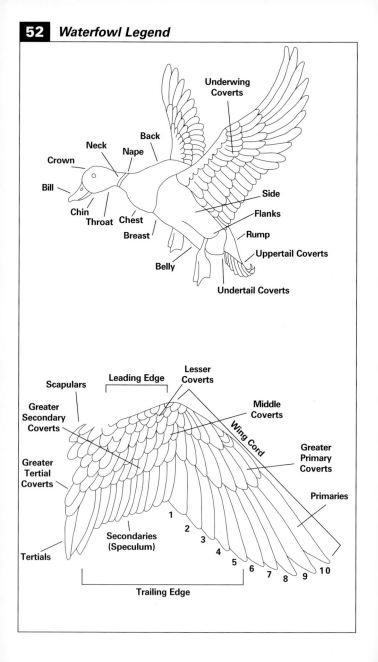

Waterfowl

PUDDLE DUCKS, OR DABBLERS, get their name from the primarily shallow-water areas they inhabit. In these areas—ponds, streams, rivers, marshes, bays, bayous, and shallow lakes—puddlers tip up to feed, meaning they tip their butts in the air while their heads go under to feed on aquatic vegetation or invertebrates. Conversely, diving ducks, as you might have guessed, completely dive under the surface to reach their food. As a result, they inhabit deeper water—lakes, oceans, and deep rivers, for example. Puddle ducks are many times found on water much too deep to tip up, and divers are often found on water shallow enough to tip up, but typically, divers are in deeper water and puddlers are in shallower water. This is a good rule of thumb and can help narrow your choices when trying to identify ducks at a distance.

Another difference is the way in which these birds take flight. Puddlers, with their larger wing-to-body size, take off at more of an abrupt angle upward, often straight up. They push off the water with their wings and vault upward. Divers have smaller wing-to-body size and larger feet-to-body size, both adaptations for diving under water. In order to take off, they must get a running start along the surface while flapping rapidly to gain speed—much the same way an airplane takes off. Some divers are better at it than others, but the general takeoff pattern of divers is much lower than puddlers. For this reason, divers spend very little time on land. The typical wingbeat of divers, with their overall smaller wings than puddlers, is more rapid and can be a helpful first clue to identify ducks several hundred yards away.

Because of their great wing-to-body size, geese take off like puddle ducks for the most part; however, some of these bigger birds (swans) take a while getting air between them and the ground, often running along the water like divers. The less common water species included in this book—the coot, rails, gallinule, and crane—have longer legs that hang or dangle behind or stick out straight, and flight is never too swift, appearing to be a struggle.

A common way to identify a duck is to look at the wing. This book covers, in illustration and text, all duck wings in North America (with the exception of two incidental eider species), with a few tips for quick identification. Even if plumage does not identify a duck or if the bird looks like it does in the molt, the wing can still be used to sex, and most often age, the bird.

A technique to quickly age waterfowl can be used for virtually all ducks and geese; therefore, it is discussed here and not in the text of each bird. When in hand, observe the upper wing coverts. If the feathers are narrow, pale, worn and/or frayed at the tips, the bird is probably a juvenile. Also, be sure to check the tips of the tailfeathers—if they are notched, slightly or severely, the bird is a juvenile. Adults typically have broad, rounded, and smooth upper wing coverts and no notching on the tailfeather tips.

Waterfowl have a number of breeding and courtship behaviors and displays, but many overlap. Many ducks, such as mallards and other puddle ducks, perform antagonistic three, four, and multibird flights that involve one female being hounded by several males. They follow her relentlessly, biting and striking one another and trying to force her down where they can attempt copulation. Ducks are polygamous, but many form pair bonds well before reaching the breeding grounds.

Other displays are the head-toss of the goldeneyes; the quick takeoff and landing of the bufflehead; head bobbing, common to many species; and so on. Many of the pair bonds are formed as a result of similar courtship flights. They can be so similar that a description of the breeding display for each species would be beyond the scope of this field guide.

Puddle Ducks

Puddle duck taking off

Puddle duck tipping up

MALLARD *(Anas platyrhynchos)*

Nicknames	Greenhead (male), Susie (female)
Average Size and Weight	23″ to 24″ — 2 to 3 lbs

Description

- Mallards are the most common duck in North America. The male (drake) has an iridescent green head, yellow bill, and white ring around the neck. The chest is maroon, and the breast and belly a light gray. The back and wings are gray/brown; the rump is dark green/black, and undertail coverts are black. The tailfeathers are white, with one to three black curls at the tip. Legs of both sexes are varying shades of orange.

- The susie is mottled brown, with a light brown head and dark streaking through the head and on the crown. The bill is orange with black mottling. Its chest is a dark brown in comparison to the lighter breast and belly.

- Both sexes have large blue/violet wing speculum edged on each side with white. On drakes, this white does not extend into the tertial coverts as it does on the female.

Distribution/Habitat

- Mallards are common throughout all four flyways and most common in the Central and Mississippi Flyways. They breed in all of the northern United States, Canada, and Alaska, with highest concentrations in the prairie pothole region of the Dakotas, Manitoba, and Saskatchewan. They have moved east and now compete in many areas with black ducks for breeding, often interbreeding. Large numbers winter in the southwestern states, Arkansas, and Louisiana. Mallards have adapted to many urban areas and parks, where they often winter if open water permits.

- Typical habitat consists of shallow water areas to make food accessible by tipping up. Small to large lakes, ponds, marshes, swamps, flooded timber, and other flooded and dry crop fields attract mallards.

Food

- Aquatic plants (smartweeds, pondweeds, canary grass, etc.) and invertebrates, and a number of agricultural grains, such as corn, wheat, and rice.

Voice

- Most vocal of ducks. Hens make the recognizable quack, as well as 3-, 5-, and 7-note series of the basic *quack*, emphasizing the first notes and drifting off with the last notes. Both utter low feed chuckles of *tuk-a-tuk-a*. Males are quite silent except for chuckles and a low, nasal *whank* with a slight whistle in it.

Flock Information

- Small flocks of 3 to 7 birds early in the season, increasing to 40, 50, and much more during migration, typically in a varied "V" or "U" shape. Sights of thousands of mallards circling like a tornado over crop fields are common in late fall.

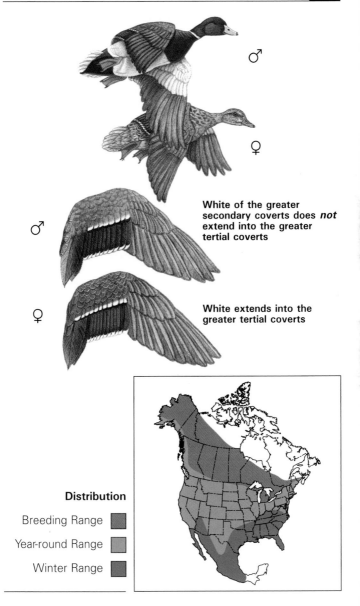

♂

♀

White of the greater
secondary coverts does *not*
extend into the greater
tertial coverts

♂

♀

White extends into the
greater tertial coverts

Distribution

Breeding Range

Year-round Range

Winter Range

MOTTLED DUCK *(Anas fulvigula)*

Nicknames   Black duck, Florida duck

Average Size and Weight 21″ to 23″ — 2 to 3 lbs

Description

- Mottled ducks are commonly confused with hen mallards and black ducks, and one of the best identification methods is location. Mottled ducks are primarily found along the southern coast of Florida and the southeastern Gulf States.
- Plumage is a dark brown mottling that is darker than the hen mallard's and lighter than the black duck. The bill is yellow, similar to the black's, and the blue/green speculum is edged in back with a more pronounced white stripe than the black duck; the cheeks and throat are lighter and lack the dark striping of the black. The feet of both sexes are orange. Female mottled ducks are similar except for the orange and black mottled bill.

Distribution/Habitat

- Mottled ducks do not migrate as other waterfowl do, however, they do move inland in the fall for food. Typical habitat is small marshes and flooded and dry crop fields; they can be found in saltwater estuaries and other brackish water, but mostly inhabit freshwater.

Food

- While they feed on aquatic plants, grasses, and grains, their prime food is animal matter, such as mollusks, fish, snails, nymphs, and other insects.

Voice

- Similar to mallards.

Flock Information

- Consist of 2, 3, or up to a dozen birds, but rarely in large flocks like mallards.

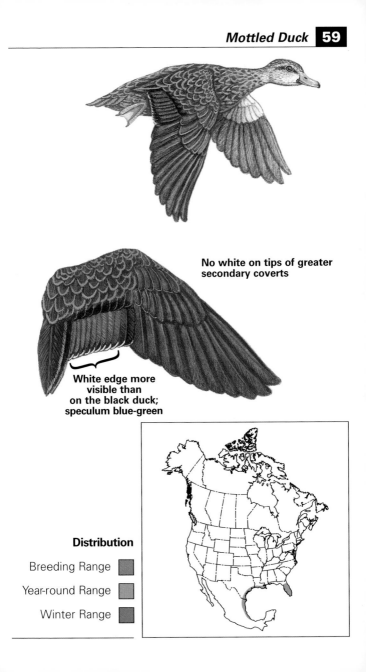

No white on tips of greater secondary coverts

White edge more visible than on the black duck; speculum blue-green

Distribution

Breeding Range

Year-round Range

Winter Range

AMERICAN BLACK DUCK *(Anas rubripes)*

Nicknames   Black, Black mallard, Red leg

Average Size and Weight   21″ to 23″ — 2½ to 3½ lbs

Description

- Black ducks are often confused with hen mallards in North America and often with mottled ducks in the mottled duck's range. This mallard-sized duck is overall dark brown, appearing almost black, with distinguishable white/silver underwing linings contrasting with the dark body. This contrast is much greater in black ducks than in hen mallards. The head is lighter brown with fine brown streaks on the cheek and throat and a dark streak going through the eye and crown.

- All dark body feathers are edged, to one degree or another, with light buff. The bill is yellow in adult drakes and olive in females with some black mottling. The male's legs tend to be brighter orange than the female's, but for the most part, sexes are nearly identical and can only be determined by wing measurements. The speculum is a deep, iridescent violet/blue and rarely edged on the bottom with light white. The front edge is bordered in black and is thus easy to differentiate from the mallard's.

Distribution

- Black ducks are primarily a bird of the East—from Michigan to Maine and the Canadian islands. They breed throughout eastern Canada and the northeastern states and migrate to the southeastern states.

- Commonly found in similar habitat as the mallard, but prefers smaller, backwater ponds, beaver ponds, streams, estuaries, and fresh and saltwater marshes. Breed on small woodland ponds where mallards are now breeding, causing interbreeding and hybrids between the two species. It is believed male mallards arrive on the breeding grounds before male blacks, establishing territories first. Hybrids often have both characteristics of mallards and blacks—sometimes just green flecking in the head or a black duck head on a mallard body.

Food

- Aquatic plants, such as eelgrass, pondweed, smartweed, etc., and invertebrates, such as mollusks and snails, in fresh and saltwater. Often found in flocks of mallards feeding in grain fields.

Voice

- Less vocal than the mallard, its similar sounds are raspier and less frequent.

Flock Information

- Loose flocks of 2 or 3 to 10 or 12 birds—not found in large mallard-sized flocks but often present in flocks of mallards. Considered by many to be the wariest of all ducks.

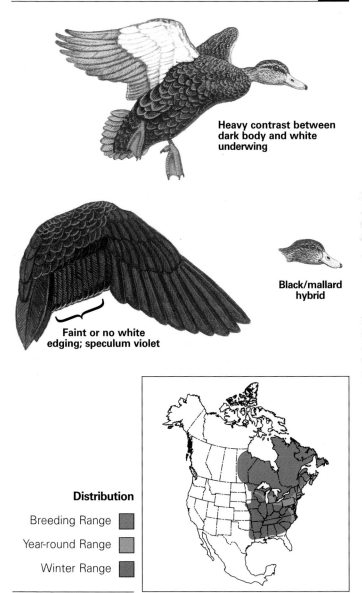

Heavy contrast between dark body and white underwing

Faint or no white edging; speculum violet

Black/mallard hybrid

Distribution

Breeding Range

Year-round Range

Winter Range

GADWALL *(Anas strepera)*

Nicknames   Gray duck, Gray mallard

Average Size and Weight   19″ to 21″ — 1½ to 2½ lbs

Description

- Gadwalls can be confused with hen mallards, especially early in the fall. Later in the season, males get their gray/brown head and back feathers; a dark, charcoal chest contrasts with the white breast and belly. The male's bill is all black or nearly black with light orange edging; the female's bill is orange with black splotches or spots—these spots are not present on the male's bill. The male's undertail coverts are black; black chest feathers are edged with white, and the sides are heavily vermiculated. Females are overall mottled brown, like the hen mallard but smaller in size. The breast is lighter, which helps distinguish it from the hen mallard.

- The best identification characteristic is the white on a portion of the speculum on the trailing edge of the wing. The wigeon is the only other puddle duck to have a white patch on the wing, but the wigeon's spot is on the leading edge. Male wings have much more russet and black on the upper wing coverts than the female, but it is important to note that females most often have black or russet on their wings, just not as much as on the male wing.

- Juveniles are mottled much like the hens.

Distribution/Habitat

- Gadwalls have responded tremendously to the North American Waterfowl Management Plan (NAWMP). They are common throughout the Pacific, Central, and Mississippi Flyways and present in the Atlantic Flyway. Highest numbers are in the Central Flyway since most gadwalls are hatched in the prairie pothole region, but they breed throughout Canada and portions of Alaska and the northern United States. Gadwalls winter heavily in Louisiana and most of the other Gulf States.

- They prefer small water, such as potholes, marshes, small lakes, and fresh and salt-water streams and estuaries.

Food

- Similar aquatic plants and invertebrates as mallards. Often found feeding in agricultural fields with mallards.

Voice

- A hoarse, poor imitation of a hen mallard call is made by the hen gadwall—*caak-cak-cak-cak*, and the male sometimes utters a low, nasal *ceck*.

Flock Information

- Small flocks up to a dozen or more, often with other puddlers. Approaching gadwalls can be tough to recognize, but look for that white in the inner portion of the speculum.

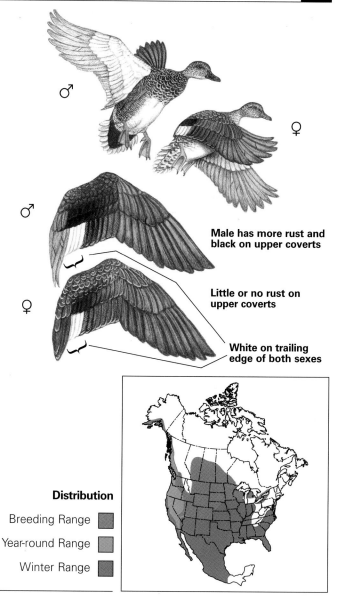

♂

♀

♂

♀

Male has more rust and black on upper coverts

Little or no rust on upper coverts

White on trailing edge of both sexes

Distribution

Breeding Range

Year-round Range

Winter Range

BLUE-WINGED TEAL *(Anas discors)*
CINNAMON TEAL *(Anas cyanoptera)*

Nicknames Bluewing; Red teal

Average Size and Weight 14″ to 15″ — ½ to 1 lb

Description

- Two of the smallest puddle ducks, blue-winged and cinnamon teal are very similar to the green-winged teal during much of the fall because nuptial plumage is typically achieved in late fall and early winter. The bluewing male has a slate blue/purple head and characteristic white facial crescent. His bill is long and black; the tan chest, breast, and belly are dotted in black. A white patch rests in front of the black rump and tail. For both sexes, observe the wings for a light to deep blue shoulder patch—similar to the shoveler, but the wing cord is shorter on the bluewing. Female bluewings are mottled brown overall, like the greenwing, but the blue wing patch gives her away.

- Male cinnamon teal are cinnamon/rust over the entire body, with light orange stripes down the scapular feathers, and orange feet. The bill is long, black, and shaped more like a miniature shoveler bill.

- In both species, most of the male's speculum is iridescent green and the female's is a dull green. Both females resemble each other too closely to identify, so identification is easier by location. Male wings have solid white outer vanes on the greater secondary coverts, while the same feathers on females are spotted with more dark than white.

Distribution/Habitat

- Bluewings are common in the Central and Mississippi Flyways and present in the Pacific and Atlantic Flyways. Breeding occurs all over Canada, parts of Alaska, and primarily in the prairie potholes of southern Canada and northcentral U.S. They leave in early September for wintering grounds on the Gulf States, Mexico, and South America. They prefer similar small water and mudflat habitat as greenwings.

- Cinnamon teal are found primarily in the Pacific and Central Flyways. Most breed in Utah's Salt Lake area and the West Coast states. They leave early for wintering grounds in Mexico and Central and South America and occupy similar habitat as other teals.

Food

- Both species feed on seeds of submergent and emergent vegetation and other aquatic grasses.

Voice

- Females of both species often utter higher-pitched *quacking* in a similar cadence to the mallard. Male bluewings tend to *peep*, or *seeel*, while cinnamon males offer a lower *chuk-chuk-chuk*.

Flock Information

- Both species fly in similar fast, synchronized, zigzag fashion as the green-winged teal, but number of birds in each flock is less.

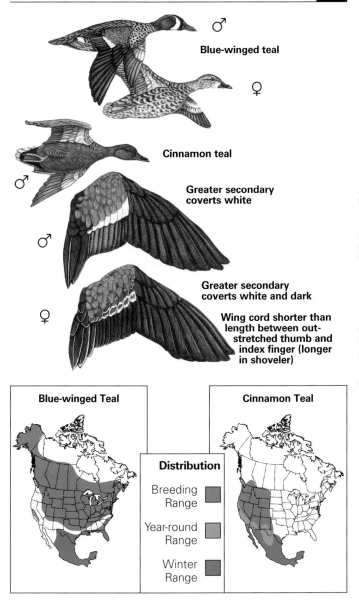

♂
Blue-winged teal
♀

Cinnamon teal

♂

Greater secondary coverts white

♂

Greater secondary coverts white and dark

♀

Wing cord shorter than length between out-stretched thumb and index finger (longer in shoveler)

Blue-winged Teal

Cinnamon Teal

Distribution

Breeding Range

Year-round Range

Winter Range

GREEN-WINGED TEAL *(Anas crecca)*

Nicknames   Greenwing

Average Size and Weight   13″ to 15″ — ½ to 1 lb

Description

- Greenwings are the smallest of all North American ducks and one of the fastest in flight. Adult males have a rusty/chestnut head with a green eye patch that extends back to the nape and is lined on the bottom with yellow. Its bill is gray and the chest tan and spotted with brown; the gray sides (vermiculated with white) and the chest are separated with a short, vertical white stripe. The belly is white with a black vertical stripe near each foot. The back and wings are brown, with a noticeable iridescent green speculum. Females are overall mottled brown with a light belly and green speculum.
- Sexes can be determined when both look similar during early fall by examining the most distal tertial feather; on males, a black stripe runs the length of the feather and is distinct from the rest of the brown feather, whereas on females, this stripe becomes washed out and blends in with the brown of the feather.
- Both sexes have similar mottling until later in the fall and winter when males reach full nuptial plumage. Juveniles resemble the female.

Distribution/Habitat

- Greenwings breed throughout much of Canada and the prairie pothole region and are common ducks in the Pacific, Central, and Mississippi Flyways, and relatively common in the Atlantic. Winter range includes much of the Southwest and Rocky Mountain states, Mexico, and Central and South America. They migrate later than blue-winged teal, often waiting well into the fall to depart.
- Marshes, potholes, and sloughs are preferred; however, larger lakes and coastal flats and estuaries are common sites for greenwings.

Food

- Seeds of both emergent and submergent vegetation in shallow water or mudflats.

Voice

- Males make *peeps* or *crick-et* calls, while females sometimes make a hurried, high-pitched series of *quacks*.

Flock Information

- Flocks of greenwings can number from 10 or 15 to 50 or more. Distinctive tight flight formation and synchronized, erratic, zigzag flight, sometimes at very high speed, make this little duck recognizable from quite a distance.

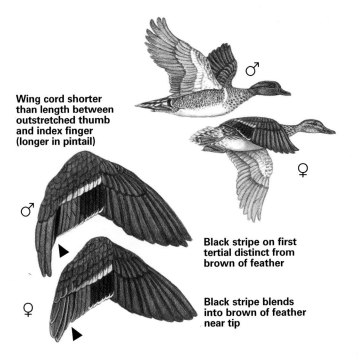

Wing cord shorter than length between outstretched thumb and index finger (longer in pintail)

♂

♀

♂

♀

Black stripe on first tertial distinct from brown of feather

Black stripe blends into brown of feather near tip

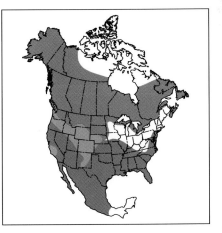

Distribution

Breeding Range

Year-round Range

Winter Range

AMERICAN WIGEON *(Anas americana)*

Nicknames   Baldpate

Average Size and Weight   17″ to 20″ — 1½ to 2 lbs

Description

- Like the gadwall, the wigeon has a white patch on the wing, although larger and located on the upper coverts, or leading edge, of the wing. On males, this white patch is a sure giveaway during flight, and it is even visible on the female.

- Wigeon have a short, light blue bill with black tip and base. The male's head is light brown with small black streaks; an iridescent green eye patch extends back to the nape; and the crown is cream/white and lacking any marking—hence the nickname "baldpate." The chest, back, and sides are a light chestnut/pink with black vermiculations and form a distinct border to the white breast and belly. The rump and undertail coverts are black, and two or three longer, pointed spikes extend out the tip of the tail. The speculum is mostly black with some green iridescence. Tertials are long, black, pointed, and edged with white.

- Females are similar but lack the white crown and green eye patch. Similar chestnut/pink feathers are on the chest, sides, and back, but they appear more mottled. Breast and belly are white, and the rump is a mottled brown. The white patch of the female's wing is less distinct than the male's. Feet of both sexes are blue/gray. Juveniles resemble hens.

Distribution/Habitat

- Wigeon are abundant in the Pacific, Central, and Mississippi Flyways and present in the Atlantic Flyway. They breed throughout central Canada and Alaska, the prairie potholes, and northwestern states. They winter along the West Coast, southern California, Gulf States, Louisiana, and Mexico.

- Found on small freshwater marshes, potholes, lakes, and fresh and saltwater bays, estuaries, and other coastal waters.

Food

- Primarily plant roots, stems, and leaves of wild celery, sedges, pondweed, wigeon grass, and other aquatic vegetation. They often sit with flocks of diving ducks in open water and steal uprooted vegetation, such as wild celery, that divers are foraging.

Voice

- Males give a soft, three-note whistle, *wew-WEW-wew*, emphasizing the second note.

Flock Information

- Flocks of several to 20 or more birds. Wings are narrow and pointed, and their aerial acrobatics give their flight the appearance of a large teal. A close cousin, the Eurasian wigeon, is occasionally seen mixed in with flocks of American wigeon along each coast. The male is more gray with a rusty head and cream crown.

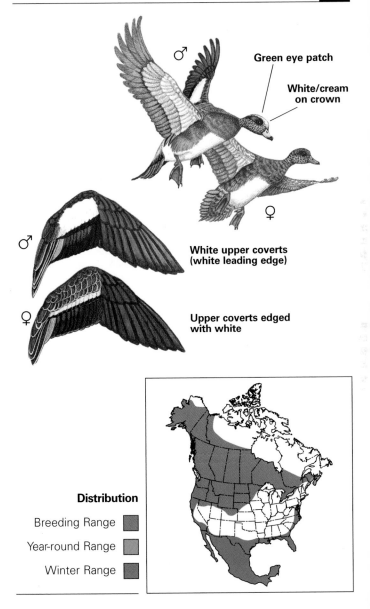

♂

Green eye patch

White/cream
on crown

♀

♂ White upper coverts
(white leading edge)

♀ Upper coverts edged
with white

Distribution

Breeding Range

Year-round Range

Winter Range

NORTHERN SHOVELER *(Anas clypeata)*

Nicknames — Spoonbill, Spoonie, Trash duck

Average Size and Weight — 18″ to 20″ — 1½ to 2 lbs

Description

- The shoveler has an unfortunate reputation of tasting bad because it strains water and mud for vegetation and aquatic insects. However, it eats much of the same foods as many other puddle ducks.

- The bill is black on males and orange with black splotching on females. Adult males in nuptial plumage have a dark green head, white breast, and rusty sides and belly; the back is gray brown. Both sexes have orange feet and a wing design nearly identical to the blue-winged teal, but the wing cord is longer on the shoveler. Tertials of males have white stripes running down the inner vane; the blue on the female's upper wing coverts is very limited, with most of these feathers edged with a light cream. Adult males have iridescent green on at least half of the feathers in their speculum, while these feathers on females are dull and noniridescent. Shoveler wings are noticeably larger than blue-winged and cinnamon teal wings; they are the only North American duck with a white rachis on all primaries of both species.

- Females and immatures are mottled brown and resemble female mallards. Male shovelers reach nuptial plumage in the winter, so many birds seen during hunting season resemble the hen.

Distribution/Habitat

- Shovelers are common in the Central and Pacific Flyways and present in the Mississippi and Atlantic Flyways. Most birds breed in the central Canadian prairies and into Alaska, and all of the prairie potholes and northwestern United States, with heaviest concentrations in the prairie potholes of Saskatchewan and Alberta. They winter along all Gulf States, but primarily the Southwest and Mexico.

- Commonly found on lakes, ponds, marshes, potholes, and similar fresh and saltwater habitat.

Food

- With their large namesake bill, they sift for aquatic plant debris and aquatic invertebrates, insects, and other animal matter. They often feed in circular groups, straining water stirred by the other ducks.

Voice

- Female shoveler's call resembles the hen mallard's.

Flock Information

- Often confused with mallards in flight, but flight tends to be more erratic. A *who-who-who* sound is often made with the wings, especially when taking off. Flock numbers are small, usually 5 to 10, and flight is swift.

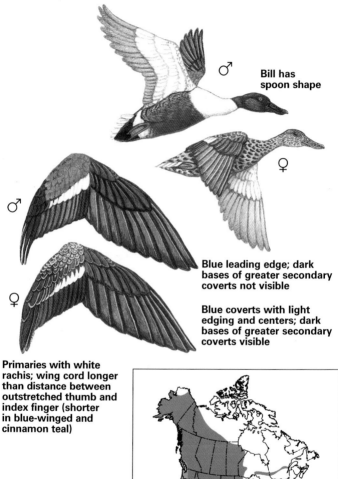

Bill has spoon shape

♂

♀

♂

♀

Blue leading edge; dark bases of greater secondary coverts not visible

Blue coverts with light edging and centers; dark bases of greater secondary coverts visible

Primaries with white rachis; wing cord longer than distance between outstretched thumb and index finger (shorter in blue-winged and cinnamon teal)

Distribution

Breeding Range

Year-round Range

Winter Range

NORTHERN PINTAIL *(Anas acuta)*

Nicknames   Sprig, Sprigtail, Spiketail

Average Size and Weight   21″ to 30″ — 1½ to 2¾ lbs

Description

- Pintails are sleek, slender ducks with narrow wings and long, thin necks. The long bill is blue/gray with black running down the middle and bordering the lower mandible and tip. The male's head is chocolate brown with white extending from the chest to a tapered point on the back of each side of the neck. The nape is gray/black and leads into a fine pattern of gray and white vermiculations down the back and sides. The breast is white and rump and undertail black, with two long, thin spikes extending out from the tail—hence the name pintail. The male's wing is overall gray/brown and the speculum partly iridescent green (sometimes bronze); tertials are long and pointed, with black surrounding the rachis.

- Females are mottled brown overall with a light breast and belly, and the brown mottled wings have a noniridescent green/brown speculum. Its long neck, larger body size, and shorter but pointed tail help differentiate it from female blue-winged teals and gadwalls.

- Both sexes have blue/gray feet. Juveniles resemble females, but by late fall, juvenile males have a lighter breast and some of the color of an adult.

Distribution/Habitat

- Pintails have a wide breeding range; however, their numbers have declined somewhat despite the improved nesting conditions of the mid to late 1990s. Common in the Central and Pacific Flyways and present in the Mississippi and Atlantic Flyways, they breed throughout most of central and western Canada (Saskatchewan, Alberta), Alaska, all of the prairie pothole areas, and northwestern United States. Pintails are early migrators and winter along the West and Gulf Coasts, Mexico, and farther south.

- They prefer potholes, marshes, and other shallow water areas, switching to shore-lines, bays, and both fresh and saltwater estuaries. They also feed in large flocks or mixed in with mallards when feeding in fields.

Food

- Pintails feed on similar foods as mallards, such as stems, leaves, and roots of aquatic plants, aquatic invertebrates, insects, and a variety of grains (corn, wheat, oats, peas, lentils, etc.).

Voice

- Males often make two and three-note trilling whistles; the female offers hoarse *quacking*.

Flock Information

- Flocks number from 5 or 10 to large numbers of birds, often feeding in fields. They are wary, circling hunters several times just out of range, before making up their minds to land or leave.

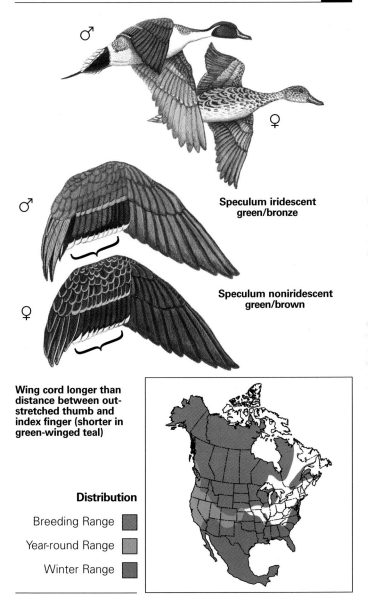

♂

♀

♂

**Speculum iridescent
green/bronze**

♀

**Speculum noniridescent
green/brown**

**Wing cord longer than
distance between out-
stretched thumb and
index finger (shorter in
green-winged teal)**

Distribution

Breeding Range

Year-round Range

Winter Range

WOOD DUCK *(Aix sponsa)*

Nicknames — Woodie, Swamp duck, Acorn duck

Average Size and Weight — 18″ to 20″ — 1 to 2 lbs

Description

- Wood ducks are the most colorful waterfowl in North America—their name in Latin means "duck in wedding dress."

- Males sport a crested green and purple head with two white lines running from the multicolored bill and behind the eye to the crest. A white chin and throat extend up in a "U" shape on the cheek; the eye is red with red eye ring. The maroon chest is flecked with white and separated from the sides by white, then black vertical bars. The ochre sides have black vermiculations and black and white tips; the breast is white, and the back and long tail are dark purple/black.

- The female's head is gray/brown with a small crest, gray bill, white chin, throat, and eye patch. Its back is dark brown/gray, and chest and sides brown with cream markings. The breast is cream/white, the tail long and gray. Both sexes have pale yellow legs and feet. Juveniles begin to resemble adults by early fall.

- Both sexes have dark brown wings and white frosting on the outer vanes of the last several primaries. The greater wing coverts are square-shaped and deep blue, while the male's may include more bronze. The secondaries are a slightly iridescent deep blue; the tips of the secondaries are thinly edged in white on males, forming a line across the bottom; on females, this white is a teardrop shape. Black tertials are the same length as the secondaries.

Distribution/Habitat

- Woodies are common in the Atlantic and Mississippi Flyways and present in the Central and Pacific Flyways. They breed throughout most of their northern range, in small holes in trees or manmade nest boxes (helping the population rebound from near extinction). They winter along the East Coast and southeastern Gulf States.

- Woodies prefer small backwater areas, such as flooded timber, swamps, rivers, ponds, potholes, and small lakes.

Food

- Primary food is acorns, eaten by tipping up or scurrying on land to fill up and return to water. Other foods are seeds, nuts, wild rice, and aquatic vegetation (duckweed, pondweed, etc.) and insects.

Voice

- Males utter soft squeaks; females make a high-pitched squealing *wheeeek-wheeeeek* or *geeeee* that gives them away before seeing them.

Flock Information

- Flocks are 4 to 15 birds, but roost on small, backwater areas in large numbers. They twist and turn to dodge limbs and trees. The long, rectangular shape and tail are good identifiers in low light.

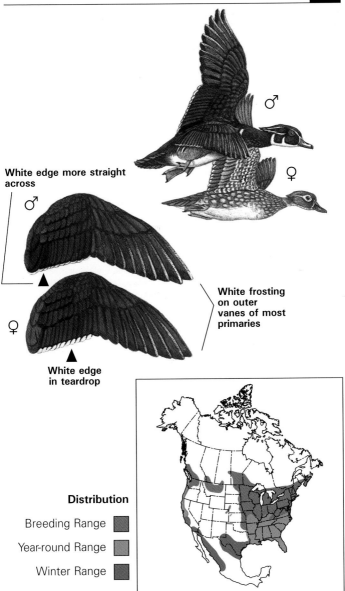

White edge more straight across

♂

♀

White frosting on outer vanes of most primaries

♀

White edge in teardrop

Distribution

Breeding Range

Year-round Range

Winter Range

BLACK-BELLIED WHISTLING DUCK
(Dendrocygna autumnalis)
FULVOUS WHISTLING DUCK
(Dendrocygna bicolor)

Nicknames	Black-bellied tree duck, Red-bellied whistling duck
	Fulvous tree duck, Squealer
Average Size and Weight	18″ to 20″—1½ to 2½ lbs (black-bellied)
	16″ to 18″—1 to 2 lbs (fulvous)

Description, Distribution/Habitat, Food, Voice, Flock Information

- Plumages are similar between the two sexes (males tend to be brighter than females). They have the most erect posture of all ducks. The head and upper neck are gray, crown rust, and bill bright orange/red. The neck, chest, and back are cinnamon/brown. A black streak runs up the back of the neck, and the breast and belly are black. The undertail coverts are black and white, and the long legs are pink.

- The wing is black with white on all of the greater and middle wing coverts, and the lesser coverts and tertials are olive.

- Black-bellied whistling ducks are found in the extreme southwestern United States and Mexico. They tend to perch in trees and are found along the banks and shallow areas of rivers, marshes, or ponds. They graze in flocks for grain, such as corn and sorghum, and other grasses and insects.

- They are quite vocal, whistling *pe-che-che-che* and *wa-chu-whe-whe* calls. Their slow, erratic flight and long legs hanging out back make them appear gangly.

- Fulvous whistling ducks have a long, blue/gray bill, legs, and feet. The flat crown and head, chest, and belly are tan/rust, and the back dark brown. The front and sides of the neck are white with brown streaking. Black runs from the back of the head down to the back; the dark tail and rump are separated by a white "V" that is visible in flight. The tan feathers on the side are edged in white. The overall appearance, with long neck and legs, is goose-like. Sexes are similar (females a bit duller), and wings of both are dark brown with faint edging on coverts.

- Fulvous whistling ducks gather in large flocks, flying in a gangly fashion similar to the black-bellied whistling duck. They can be found throughout the extreme south and southeast U.S., from Florida to Mexico. Their habitat and food preferences are similar to the black-bellied whistling duck. The call is a whistling *c-weeoo*.

Black-bellied Whistling Duck
Olive upper coverts;
greater secondary
and primary coverts white

Fulvous Whistling Duck

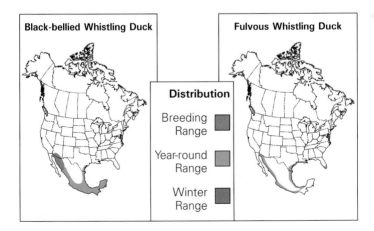

Black-bellied Whistling Duck

Fulvous Whistling Duck

Distribution

Breeding Range

Year-round Range

Winter Range

Mallard Phases Through Molt

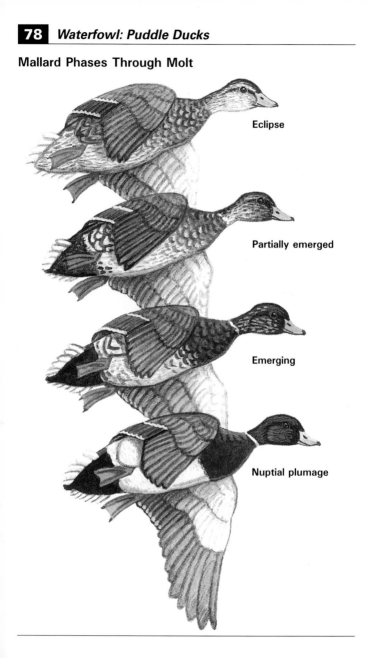

Eclipse

Partially emerged

Emerging

Nuptial plumage

Diving Ducks

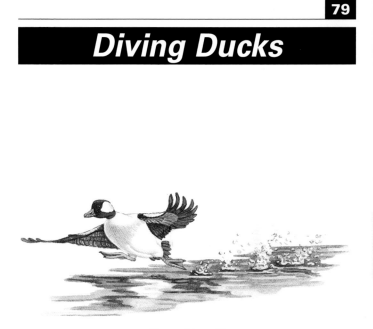

Diver taking off

REDHEAD *(Aythya americana)*

Nicknames   Pochard

Average Size and Weight   18″ to 20″—1½ to 2½ lbs

Description

- Redheads are commonly confused with canvasbacks, scaup, or mallards in silhouette. Males have a rounded, red/chestnut head with yellow eye; the bill is light blue/gray with a faded white band before the black tip. The chest is black and breast and belly white or dull gray; the back is gray with fine white vermiculations, and the rump and uppertail coverts are black. By midautumn, males have red heads but the body is typically still mottled brown from the molt.

- Females are brown and gray, with similar but duller bill color. The dark eye is surrounded by a thin circle of white, and the chin and throat are buff. The belly and breast are white.

- Legs of each sex are gray/blue, and wings are gray/brown with a light gray speculum that is lighter that the ringneck's speculum, but not as light as a scaup's. The overall wing is much darker than the canvasback. A good rule to tell the difference between redhead and canvasback wings is to examine the degree of white flecking and vermiculations. Males have more of these markings on the upper wing coverts and tertial tips than females, but canvasback females have more than redhead males, and canvasback males have so much that they appear white. The degree of white flecking, therefore, is (from most to least): male canvasback, female canvasback, male redhead, female redhead.

Distribution

- Redheads are common in the Pacific and Central Flyways and quite common in the Mississippi and Atlantic Flyways. They breed across most of the prairie pothole region of the Canadian provinces and United States, as well as in Utah. They winter heavily along the southwestern coast and most of the southern states.

- Typically found on potholes or larger lakes, bays, and estuaries—both fresh and saltwater.

Food

- Redheads dive to feed on aquatic vegetation, mainly wild celery, coontail, pondweed, duckweed, wild rice, and a variety of others. A small amount of animal matter adds to their diet.

Voice

- Males make a *purring* or *meowing* sound, similar to a cat.

Flock Information

- Fly in small flocks up to about 15 birds—more often seen as pairs or flocks of 3 to 5. They sit or fly with other divers, especially scaup and canvasbacks.

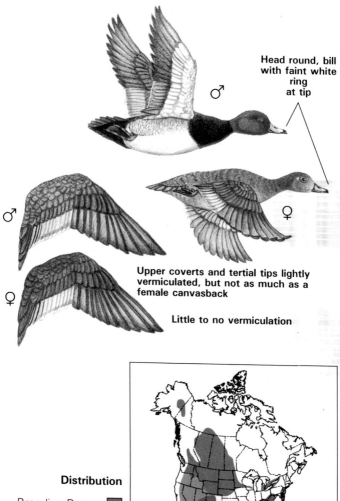

♂

Head round, bill with faint white ring at tip

♀

♂

♀

Upper coverts and tertial tips lightly vermiculated, but not as much as a female canvasback

Little to no vermiculation

Distribution

Breeding Range

Year-round Range

Winter Range

CANVASBACK *(Aythya valisineria)*

Nicknames   Can, Bullneck

Average Size and Weight   19″ to 22″ —2½ to 3½ lbs

Description

- Canvasbacks are considered by many hunters to be the king of ducks. Highly prized for table fare, they were hunted nearly to extinction in the market hunting days of the early 1900s. Closed seasons and improved nesting conditions have allowed cans to be hunted once again, although U.S. hunters are typically allowed only one bird in the bag per day.

- A big diver, cans are often confused with redheads because of similar plumage characteristics at first sight. The male's red/chestnut head is sloped and not rounded, as is the redhead's, and the bill is long, sloping, and black. Its neck is long and thick, the chest black, and breast and belly white. The gray back is so heavily flecked with white that it appears overall white in flight. The wings are likewise nearly white.

- The female is brown overall but has the same sloping head and bill features of the male. Feathers are buff around the eye, and the breast and belly are white with gray/brown color on the sides and back.

- The feet of both are gray/blue. The rump and undertail coverts are black on the male or dark brown on the female. Immature males have more gray on the back and wings as the fall progresses.

Distribution/Habitat

- Canvasback numbers are still rising, responding well to years of improved habitat and protected status. They are common throughout all flyways and breed in Alaska, central and western Canada, all of the prairie potholes, and some western states. They migrate south along the West Coast and Central Flyway and southeast from Saskatchewan and Manitoba to the Great Lakes states and along the Atlantic Coast —often to a traditional wintering area at Chesapeake Bay.

- They prefer prairie marshes, potholes, lakes, rivers, bays, and large open water— both fresh and salt.

Food

- Primary food is wild celery (Latin name, *Vallisneria,* is the genus of wild celery) but also feed on pondweed, bulrush, coontail, and other aquatic plants, as well as aquatic invertebrates or fish. They dive up to 20 or 30 feet for food, often straining mud for seeds.

Voice

- Mostly silent, although males often utter low *skrrll* sounds.

Flock Information

- Seen in small flocks during hunting season but raft in large numbers on open water during migration and on wintering areas. Flight is direct and fast, often exceeding speeds of 70 mph.

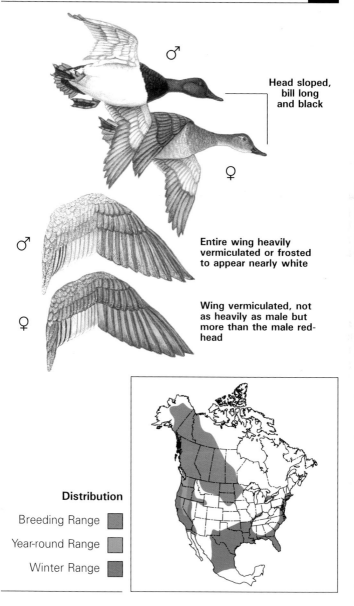

Head sloped, bill long and black

Entire wing heavily vermiculated or frosted to appear nearly white

Wing vermiculated, not as heavily as male but more than the male redhead

Distribution

Breeding Range

Year-round Range

Winter Range

RING-NECKED DUCK *(Aythya collaris)*

Nicknames Ringbill, Ring-billed duck, Ringneck, Blackjack

Average Size and Weight 16″ to 18″—1¼ to 2 lbs

Description

- Ringnecks get their name from the faint crimson ring around the neck of the male. This ring is not visible in flight and hardly visible in hand; therefore they are often referred to as "ringbills" because of the white ring around the bill, near the black tip. Another white stripe also borders the base of the gray bill on the male.

- The male's head is black with purple iridescence and a pointy crown; the eye is yellow. The chest is black and comes to a distinct break across the white breast and belly. The back, rump, and undertail coverts are black, and at rest, the white of the breast makes a triangle with the black chest, wing, and back. The sides are white with fine gray vermiculations.

- Females are tawny brown with a thin white circle around the eye and a light cheek and throat. The chest and sides are brown, the belly white, and the back and rump dark brown. The smaller size, angular head, and wing characteristics help to separate it from the similar female redhead. Both sexes have gray/blue legs and feet. Juveniles resemble hens; but in early autumn, young males begin to display white on the bill and a darker head and chest.

- Wings of ringnecks are similar to redhead wings but are darker with contrasting lighter gray speculum. The male's secondaries are often faintly tipped in white. Both sexes can be identified from the redhead by the green iridescent tertials, the "oil spot."

Distribution/Habitat

- Ringnecks are common in the Atlantic and Mississippi Flyways and present in the Central and Pacific Flyways. They breed across most of Canada—primarily Alberta, Saskatchewan, and Manitoba—and the northern United States. They winter along the coasts—the Carolinas, Florida, and nearly all the Gulf States and Mexico.

- Ringbills frequent small, backwater marshes, floodings, ponds, swamps, and small lakes and rivers, making daily feeding trips from larger-water resting areas to small woodland lakes and floodings.

Food

- Ringnecks typically feed in only several feet of water on various aquatic vegetation, such as pondweed, coontail, wild rice, duckweed, etc.; they also eat insects and aquatic invertebrates.

Voice

- Quite silent, with the main sounds being low, guttural *skrrls.*

Flock Information

- Fly in flocks of 5 or 6 to 20 or more. Formation is bunched and varying, often synchronized; flight is fast. Flight often announced by a loud *swooshing* sound made by air moving through the wings like a jet plane.

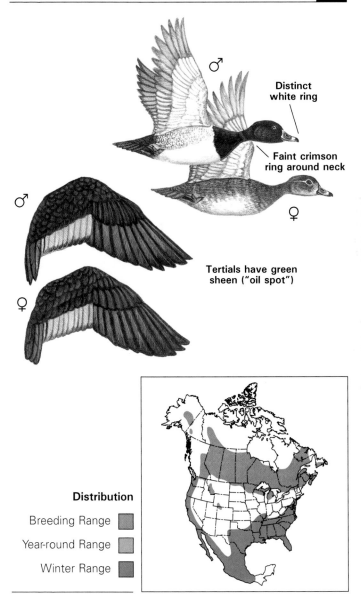

♂

Distinct
white ring

Faint crimson
ring around neck

♂

♀

Tertials have green
sheen ("oil spot")

♀

Distribution

Breeding Range

Year-round Range

Winter Range

LESSER SCAUP *(Aythya affinis)*

Nicknames Bluebill

Average Size and Weight 15½" to 18"—1 to 2 lbs

Description

- There are two scaup species of North America, lesser and greater. Lesser scaup are commonly referred to as "bluebills" because of the male's light blue bill color.

- Males have black heads with purple and green hues. Typically, lessers have a green sheen and greaters have a purple sheen, but that should not be used as the main identifying characteristic. The chest, rump, and undertail coverts are black, and the belly white. The back is white with black vermiculations, appearing whiter as the bird reaches nuptial plumage.

- Females are similar, with gray bills, brown heads, sides, back, and rump. A white facial patch rests around the base of the bill, and the belly is white. Both sexes have blue/gray feet. Juveniles resemble females, and young males often have a portion of the white facial patch, and thus often mistaken for a hen.

- The differentiating characteristic between these two species is the amount of white in the wing. Lessers have white only in the speculum.

Distribution/Habitat

- Scaup breed in northern Canada, the Yukon, Alaska, and the prairie pothole region of central Canada and the northern United States. Lessers winter over the southern range of all four flyways. Both winter on the Great Lakes.

- Prefers open water—lakes, bays, and large rivers—but lessers can be found on smaller ponds, potholes, and marshes.

Food

- They feed in several to 15 or 20 feet of water on aquatic vegetation, such as wild rice, coontail, wild celery, as well as aquatic animals, such as mollusks, snails, zebra mussels, etc. Greaters feed more on mollusks, fish, and other ocean animals.

Voice

- The typical call is a low *skrrrlll*.

Flock Information

- Fly in flocks of 6 or 8 to 20 or more. Flight and wingbeats are similar to ringnecks. On staging and wintering areas, scaup sit in rafts numbering in the thousands, often with redheads and canvasbacks.

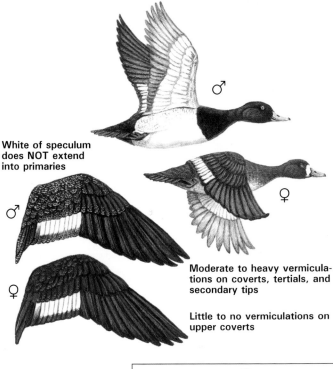

White of speculum does NOT extend into primaries

Moderate to heavy vermiculations on coverts, tertials, and secondary tips

Little to no vermiculations on upper coverts

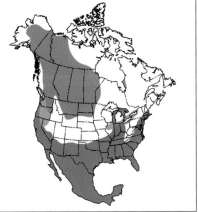

Distribution

Breeding Range

Year-round Range

Winter Range

GREATER SCAUP *(Aythya marila)*

Nicknames   Bluebill, Broadbill

Average Size and Weight   16″ to 19″—1½ to 3 lbs

Description

- Greater scaup are also nicknamed "bluebills" because of the male's light blue bill color but are more commonly called "broadbills" due to the larger bill.
- Males have black heads with purple and green hues. The chest, rump, and under-tail coverts are black, and the belly white. The backs are white with black vermiculations, appearing whiter as the bird reaches nuptial plumage.
- Females are similar, with gray bills, brown heads, sides, back, and rump. A white facial patch rests around the base of the bill, and the belly is white. Both sexes have blue/gray feet. Juveniles resemble females, and young males often have a portion of the white facial patch, and thus often mistaken for a hen.
- The differentiating characteristic between these two species is the amount of white in the wing. Greaters have white in the speculum and extending into the first seven or eight primaries.

Distribution/Habitat

- Scaup breed in northern Canada, the Yukon, Alaska, and the prairie pothole region of central Canada and the northern United States. Greaters winter primarily in the Atlantic Flyway and along the East Coast. Both winter on the Great Lakes.
- Prefer open water—lakes, bays, and large rivers. Greater scaup are more likely to be found along the tidal bays and inlets of the Atlantic, and sometimes Pacific, Oceans.

Food

- They feed in several to 15 or 20 feet of water on aquatic vegetation, such as wild rice, coontail, wild celery, as well as aquatic animals, such as mollusks, snails, zebra mussels, etc. Greaters feed more on mollusks, fish, and other ocean animals.

Voice

- The typical call is a low *skrrrlll*.

Flock Information

- Fly in flocks of 6 or 8 to 20 or more. Flight and wingbeats are similar to ringnecks. On staging and wintering areas, scaup sit in rafts numbering in the thousands, often with redheads and canvasbacks.

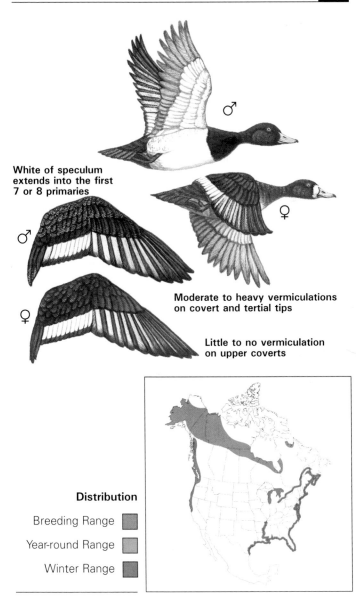

White of speculum
extends into the first
7 or 8 primaries

♂

♀

♀

Moderate to heavy vermiculations
on covert and tertial tips

Little to no vermiculation
on upper coverts

Distribution

Breeding Range

Year-round Range

Winter Range

COMMON GOLDENEYE *(Bucephala clangula)*

Nicknames   Whistler

Average Size and Weight   16″ to 19″—2 to 3¼ lbs
(males noticeably larger)

Description

- Common goldeneyes are found in all four flyways, whereas a close cousin, the Barrow's goldeneye, is primarily found along each coast.
- The male is chunky with a short, black bill and a green/black, rather pointed head; a small white circle sits at the base of the bill and below the yellow eye. The neck, large chest, belly, sides, and upper back are white and extremely visible at a distance. Its back is mostly black with white striping on the scapulars, and the rump and tail are black.
- Females are smaller and have a gray, stubby bill, often with a pale orange tip. The angular head is chocolate brown with no white facial spot; chest is lighter and belly white, with gray sides and darker brown/gray back and tail.
- Male wings are black and white with a large white shoulder patch that does not extend to the bend of the wing (as it does in the smaller bufflehead wing). The white extends down over the middle coverts and most of the speculum. It is similar on females, but the white on the upper coverts is grayer and less distinct. The wing cord is at least as long as the length between the outstretched thumb and index finger (much shorter on buffleheads). The feet of both sexes are yellow/orange.
- Wind through their wings makes a whistling sound—very audible on quiet mornings, giving them their nickname, "whistler."

Distribution/Habitat

- Present in all four flyways, they are common visitors to the Mississippi and Atlantic Flyways, especially the Great Lakes and along the East Coast. They breed throughout most of Canada and Alaska and winter on the Great Lakes, along the coasts, and as far south as is necessary to find open water and food. They are often among the last to migrate.
- Found on lakes and bays in relatively open fresh and coastal waters.

Food

- Wild celery, pondweeds, and other aquatic plants, as well as aquatic invertebrates, fish, and insects.

Voice

- Quite silent, although males do make a shrill *zeeeee-at* while performing head-toss displays during breeding season and occasionally during the fall.

Flock Information

- Fly in flocks of 5 to 15 or 20 and rest in similar-sized flocks or large rafts of 100 or 200 birds, and their flight is steady. They are not as sociable as other divers, making them a challenge to hunt.

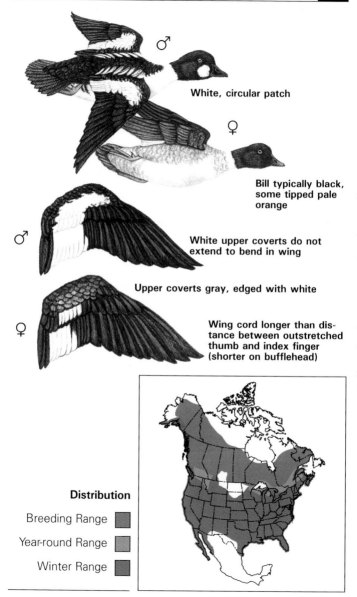

White, circular patch

Bill typically black, some tipped pale orange

♂ White upper coverts do not extend to bend in wing

Upper coverts gray, edged with white

♀ Wing cord longer than distance between outstretched thumb and index finger (shorter on bufflehead)

Distribution

Breeding Range

Year-round Range

Winter Range

BARROW'S GOLDENEYE *(Bucephala islandica)*

Nicknames   Whistler, Rocky Mountain goldeneye

Average Size and Weight   16″ to 19″—1¼ to 2½ lbs

Description

- The Barrow's goldeneye, especially the female, is often confused with the common goldeneye because of similar plumage. The head of the male rises abruptly from the short, black bill and rounds off more than the angled head of the common. The head is black with a purple sheen instead of green, and the white patch on the face is in a crescent shape, extending up in front of the yellow eye. The neck, upper back, and belly are all white, but the black back extends down the white sides farther than on the common. The scapular feathers are blacker, creating smaller, white spots and not stripes as on the common.

- The adult Barrow's female is nearly indistinguishable from the common female or juvenile of either species. Only in the spring breeding season does the hen have a significant amount of orange on the bill to help compare to the small yellow/orange spot on the bill of the female common goldeneye.

- The Barrow's wing is similar to the common goldeneye but lacks as much white on the upper coverts. The bases of the greater secondary coverts are black on each species, but on the Barrow's, the black extends farther toward the white tip than on the common and is therefore visible. This black base is hidden on the common. The feet of both sexes are yellow/orange.

- As with the common goldeneye, the Barrow's whistles when it flies.

Distribution/Habitat

- Barrow's can be identified in most places of North America by knowing that they are restricted to certain areas of Alaska and along the coasts. The primary range is along the northern Pacific and Atlantic Flyways, in the Rockies, and the St. Lawrence River. They spend time on woodland lakes and rivers, rapid mountain streams, and coastal bays and estuaries.

Food

- Aquatic insects (dragonfly and damselfly nymphs) and invertebrates, such as mollusks, and fish and seeds from some aquatic plants.

Voice

- Males utter soft cries and grunts but are otherwise quite silent.

Flock Information

- Most often seen in small groups of 3, 5, or a dozen birds or more. They winter in large flocks but not as large as common goldeneye flocks. The Barrow's goldeneye flight is similar to the common.

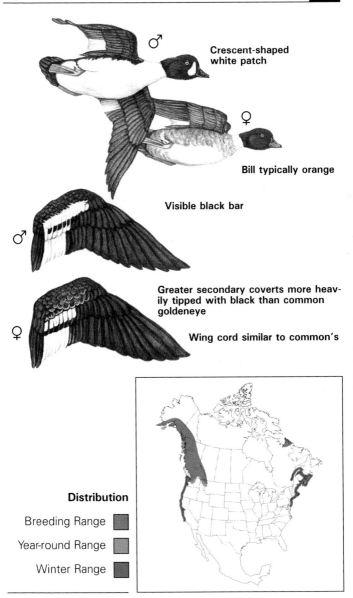

♂

Crescent-shaped
white patch

♀

Bill typically orange

Visible black bar

♂

Greater secondary coverts more heavily tipped with black than common
goldeneye

♀

Wing cord similar to common's

Distribution

Breeding Range

Year-round Range

Winter Range

BUFFLEHEAD *(Bucephala albeola)*

Nicknames   Butterball, Buffalohead

Average Size and Weight   12″ to 15″—½ to 1½ lbs

Description

- One of the smallest ducks and the smallest diving duck, the bufflehead resembles a small goldeneye. The male is a chunky, black and white bird with a short, slender gray/black bill; black head with purple, green, and bronze sheens; and a large white wedge behind the eye and extending to the back of the head. The neck, chest, belly, sides, and upper back are all white, with a black back and rump, and long, silver/gray tail. The wings are black and white, with white extending from the inner four or five secondaries up through the upper wing coverts and to the bend of the wing (similar white on the goldeneye wing does not extend to the bend). The wing cord is shorter than the distance between the outstretched thumb and index finger.
- Females are small, pale brown ducks with thin gray bills and a brown head with a white dash behind the eye. It has a light gray to white neck, sides, chest, and belly. The back, rump, and long tail are all brown. The wing is likewise dark brown/black, with only a small amount of white on the inner secondaries and greater secondary coverts.
- The male's feet are large and pink, while the female's are gray. Males gain nuptial plumage by early fall.

Distribution/Habitat

- Buffleheads are present in all flyways and are common in the Mississippi, Atlantic, and Pacific Flyways. They breed across much of Canada and Alaska, the northern Rocky Mountains, and the northwestern states. They winter primarily along the coasts and the Great Lakes, and often only as far south as is necessary to find food and open water.
- Primary habitat is lakes, ponds, and rivers, moving to coastal rivers, estuaries, and lakes on wintering grounds.

Food

- Small fish, aquatic insects (damselfly, caddis, dragonfly larvae, etc.) and aquatic invertebrates, such as shrimp and snails. Occasionally feed on aquatic plant seeds, such as pondweed and bulrush.

Voice

- Mostly silent, but females do utter low *skrrrlls*.

Flock Information

- Fly in small flocks of 2 or 3 to a dozen, but rarely more; staging flocks can be larger. Flight is steady and swift, with rapid wingbeats. Often bunch up while approaching decoys, and it is easy to hit more than one with a shot.

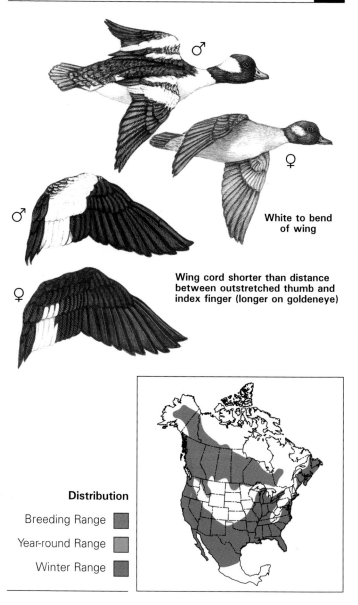

♂

♀

White to bend
of wing

Wing cord shorter than distance
between outstretched thumb and
index finger (longer on goldeneye)

♂

♀

Distribution

Breeding Range

Year-round Range

Winter Range

COMMON MERGANSER *(Mergus merganser)*

Nicknames Fish duck, Helldiver, Sawbill, Goosander

Average Size and Weight 22″ to 27″—2½ to 4½ lbs

Description

- Common mergansers are one of three merganser species in North America. Common and red-breasted mergansers are difficult to differentiate, but hoodeds are much smaller and found in different habitat. Mergansers have a unique and highly adapted slim, serrated bill to aid in catching fish—much different from the typical duck bill.
- Compared to red-breasted mergansers, commons are large divers with an orange bill that is thicker at the base and has nostrils near the center of the bill. The head on the adult male is green with no crest. The eyes and feet are dark orange/red. The male's body is more slender than the goldeneye's, with which it is also confused. The neck, sides, chest, belly, and upper back are all white, and the back is black with a dark gray tail.
- Females have a similar but duller bill and feet. The head is brown with a slight crest and distinct white throat. Its neck, chest, and belly are white; the sides, back, and tail are silver/gray. Juveniles and eclipse males resemble females.
- The large wings are black and white. The male has white on most of the upper wing coverts, which do not cover the black bases of the greater secondary coverts. These coverts cover the dark bases of the secondaries. Most tertials are long, pointed, and white with black edging. The female's wing is gray over the middle and lesser wing coverts, tertial coverts, and tertials. The greater secondary coverts are tipped with black.

Distribution/Habitat

- Common mergansers are regularly found in all flyways, breeding across most of Canada and Alaska and the northern United States, primarily the Great Lakes and Rocky Mountain states. They winter across much of the United States.
- They are found on small lakes, rivers, larger bays, and large inland lakes, as well as the coasts on saltwater bays and estuaries.

Food

- They feed in small squadrons, dipping the head below surface to spot fish before diving after them, and small fish are their primary target. Other foods include crustaceans, mollusks, and other small vertebrates and invertebrates.

Voice

- Males croak, while females utter a quick, hoarse *skrrl* or *carrr* or series of *carrrs*.

Flock Information

- Common mergansers fly in low, often single-file flocks. Wingbeats are rapid with a shallow arc (unlike a goldeneye, for example). They typically skitter along the surface longer than other divers do before taking flight. The meat is strong due to their fish diet, making them unpopular among hunters.

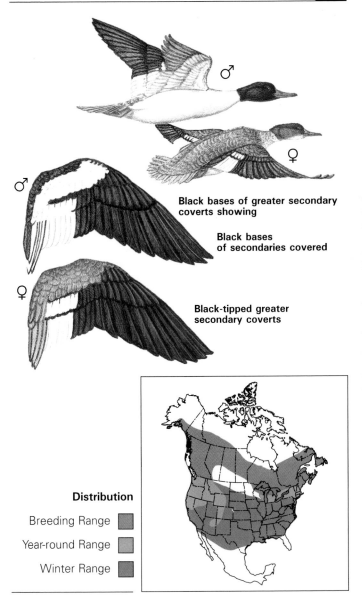

♂

♀

Black bases of greater secondary coverts showing

Black bases of secondaries covered

♂

♀

Black-tipped greater secondary coverts

Distribution

Breeding Range

Year-round Range

Winter Range

RED-BREASTED MERGANSER *(Mergus serrator)*

Nickname   Sawbill, Fish duck, Helldiver

Average Size and Weight   16″ to 18″—1½ to 2½ lbs

Description

- Red-breasted mergansers are found mainly along the ocean coasts, which is helpful in differentiating them from the similar common merganser.

- Both sexes have the thin orange, serrated bill that is a characteristic of mergansers, but it is thinner at the base, and the nostrils are closer to the base than they are on the common. The male's green head is crested, with the neck ringed in white. The chest is red/yellow with rows of black spots; the sides are gray and belly white. The black back extends down the sides somewhat, and the rump is black.

- The female's bill is duller, as are the feet. The thin, cinnamon/brown head is crested, and its throat lacks the distinct white of the common, being instead a light gray. The chest and belly are white and the sides and back gray/brown. Juveniles resemble females, and males do not reach nuptial plumage until late fall or early winter. Females and juvenile and eclipse males are virtually identical to female and juvenile commons, except for the wing.

- White covers most of the lesser and middle wing coverts of males but does not completely cover the dark bases of the greater secondary coverts, which do not completely cover the black bases of the secondaries, creating two black bars on the wing. The first three tertials are also white with black edging. Females have black/brown upper wing coverts and white greater secondary coverts with thin, black tips. The tertials are gray and black.

Distribution/Habitat

- Red-breasted mergansers are primarily found along the Pacific and Atlantic Flyways and breed from southeastern Canada and the Great Lakes across most of northern Canada and Alaska. They winter down each coast, the Gulf States, and the Great Lakes.

- They can be found on small lakes and rivers, larger bays, and large inland lakes, as well as on the ocean coasts, saltwater bays, and estuaries.

Food

- They feed in small squadrons, dipping the head below surface to spot fish before diving after them, and primarily eat small fish. Other foods include crustaceans, mollusks, and other vertebrates and invertebrates.

Voice

- Females make calls similar to the *carrr-carrr-carrr* made by female commons, as well as other croaks.

Flock Information

- Fly in similar fashion and flock formation as the common merganser, often mixed in with flocks of common mergansers where populations overlap.

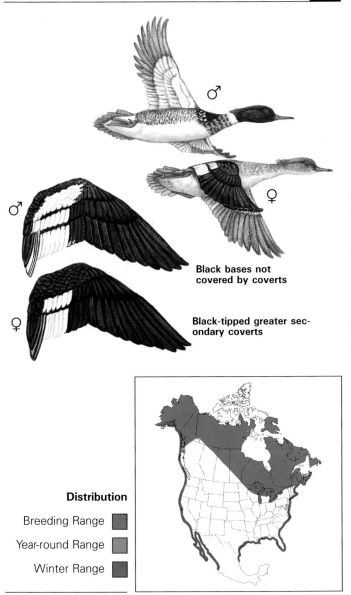

Black bases not covered by coverts

Black-tipped greater secondary coverts

Distribution

Breeding Range

Year-round Range

Winter Range

HOODED MERGANSER *(Mergus cucullatus)*

Nicknames   Hooded, Hoodie, Sawbill, Fish duck

Average Size and Weight   16″ to 19″—1¼ to 2 lbs

Description

- The smallest of the three mergansers, the hooded is most often confused with buffle-heads and wood ducks. The male's head sports thick, bushy black feathers with a large white wedge behind the eye extending back to the nape and edged in black. The thin merganser bill is black, and the eye is yellow. The amount of white showing on the head depends on whether the crest is lying down or raised. The neck and back are black, and the black on the upper back extends halfway down in two thin fingers on each side of the chest. The sides are yellow ochre with fine black vermiculations; the tail is long and brown.

- Female hoodeds have a thin, pale orange and black bill with a rust brown/gray crested head, neck, and chest. The belly is cream to white, and the sides, back, rump, and tail are dark brown. Juveniles resemble females, but males achieve nuptial colors early enough in the fall to be identifiable.

- The short black/brown wings have distinguishable long, curved black tertials with white stripes. The males have gray upper wing coverts.

Distribution/Habitat

- Hoodeds are primarily found in the Pacific, Mississippi, and Atlantic Flyways. They breed across southeastern and southwestern Canada and the northeastern and northwestern United States and the Great Lakes. The winter range includes all of the southeastern United States and along the Pacific Coast.

- Hooded mergansers are found in smaller-water areas than the other two mergansers—ponds, floodings, marshes, small lakes, and rivers. They are also found along coastal areas during winter.

Food

- Fish and other aquatic vertebrates and invertebrates, as well as frogs, salamanders, seeds of aquatic plants, and insects.

Voice

- Female utters hoarse *skrrrll*, and male utters a long, drawn out, hoarse *crrroooak*.

Flock Information

- Typical flocks are 2 or 3 to 8 or 10, making them difficult to distinguish from the similar bufflehead. Flight is steady and swift.

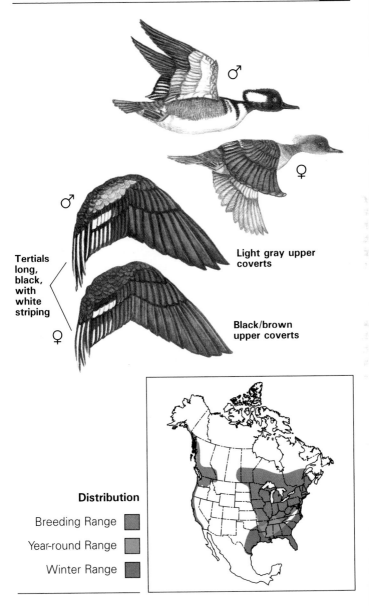

♂

♀

♂

Tertials long, black, with white striping

♀

Light gray upper coverts

Black/brown upper coverts

Distribution

Breeding Range

Year-round Range

Winter Range

RUDDY DUCK *(Oxyura jamaicensis)*

Nicknames — Bullneck, Bristletail, Bumblebee duck

Average Size and Weight — 14″ to 16″—½ to 1½ lbs

Description

- One of the smallest diving ducks, these stiff-tailed ducks are not a popular game bird during hunting season because they often prefer to swim or dive under water to evade danger.
- Males do not achieve their nuptial plumage until late winter, most often February and March, when the neck, chest, back, sides, and rump turn a deep chestnut/red. The crown becomes black, and the white cheek patch becomes more distinct. Their exceptionally wide, stocky bill turns from gray to a bright blue.
- During fall, male and juvenile ruddy ducks resemble the female, with an overall brown body and dark crown with white cheek; their bellies are a silver/white color. The female's white cheek is duller and streaked.
- The stiff tails are often carried at a 45-degree angle, and during breeding season, 90 degrees. Wings of both sexes are a similar dark brown with no white.

Distribution/Habitat

- Ruddies breed in the prairie pothole region of southcentral Canada and north-central United States, the Great Lakes, and the northwestern United States. They typically head south and west along the Pacific Coast during migration, but a good number head southwest to the Great Lakes, along the Atlantic Coast, southern states, and Mexico.
- Look for ruddy ducks on prairie potholes, small lakes and marshes, rivers, or coastal bays and estuaries.

Food

- They mainly eat vegetation—seeds of pondweeds, smartweeds, sedges—but also eat aquatic insects, especially midge and caddis larvae.

Voice

- Mostly silent, but males utter low *chuk-chuk-chuk-chuk-churrr* sounds in the spring.

Flock Information

- Typically seen as singles, pairs, or small flocks seldom greater than 10. Flight is steady and low, with a shallow arc like the common and red-breasted mergansers. A rapid wingbeat and short, chunky body gives them the look of a large bumblebee in flight.

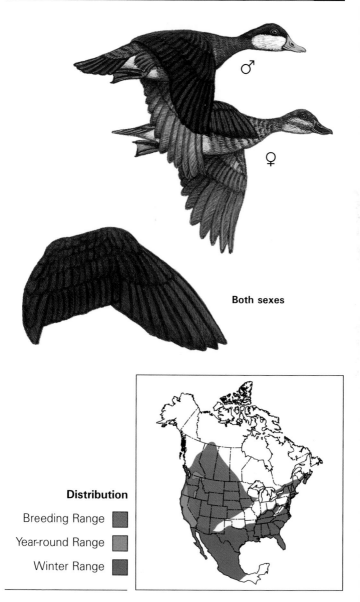

♂

♀

Both sexes

Distribution

Breeding Range

Year-round Range

Winter Range

OLDSQUAW *(Clangula hyemalis)*

Nicknames   Cockawee, Long-tailed duck

Average Size and Weight   15″ to 22″—1½ to 2½ lbs

Description

- Oldsquaws are the only sea diving ducks that have a long tail, similar to the pintail but lacking its long, thin neck.
- Male oldsquaws go through plumage changes in a similar manner as ptarmigan. Males are overall brown/black with a white cheek patch and white belly, sides, and undertail coverts during the spring and summer. The oldsquaw male in the fall hunting season is half black and half white. The head is white with a tan cheek and a dark brown patch behind the eye. The chest, lower back, and wings are black/brown, and the sides, belly, long scapular feathers, and upper back are all white, with a dark brown/black breast band. The bill is pink with black at the base, and the two brown central tailfeathers extend out 6 to 8 inches, while the next two extend out 3 to 4 inches.
- The female during late hunting season has a white head with brown crown and dash on the cheek and tan band around the neck; the chest, sides, and belly are white, and the back and wings brown. It is darker in the summer.
- Wings of males are typically black with dark brown secondaries, while the female wing is more brown, having brown upper wing and tertial coverts with tan edging. Both have gray feet.

Distribution/Habitat

- Oldsquaws are quite common along both coastal flyways and present in the Great Lakes. They breed on the extreme northern Canadian Arctic tundra and Alaska and migrate down the coasts, often wintering on the Great Lakes.
- Tundra ponds and bays on the breeding grounds; large bodies of water—oceans, large inland lakes, etc., on wintering grounds.

Food

- Blue mussels and other mollusks, crustaceans, such as shrimp and crabs, and larval insects; fish; seeds of aquatic plants on the breeding grounds. Will dive to great depths for food, sometimes exceeding 150 feet.

Voice

- Vocal and audible at great distances, males call a melodious *aw-aw-awdle-aw* and *caloo* yodels, and females utter various clucks.

Flock Information

- Irregular flock formation; small flocks during nonmigration, flying low to the water with shallow arc and swerving flight, canting this way and that, at speeds from 50 to 70 mph and more. Smaller and less chunky compared to eiders and scoters, with which they can be confused.

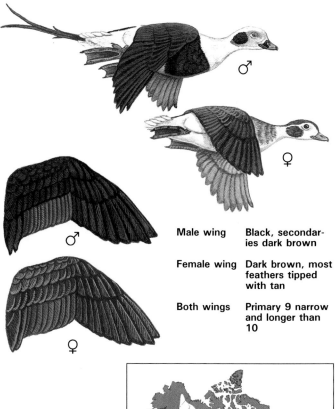

♂

♀

♂

♀

Male wing	Black, secondaries dark brown
Female wing	Dark brown, most feathers tipped with tan
Both wings	Primary 9 narrow and longer than 10

Distribution

Breeding Range

Year-round Range

Winter Range

HARLEQUIN DUCK *(Histrionicus histrionicus)*

Nicknames   Mountain duck, Painted duck

Average Size and Weight   15″ to 20″—1 to 1¾ lbs
(males bigger than females)

Description

- Second only to the wood duck for overall color and beauty, harlequin males are an overall slate blue duck with white and rust markings. A large, white crescent sits between the eye and bill and tapers to a point, turning to rust over the eye. A white dot and stripe sit behind the eye, and two vertical white stripes are on the neck and chest. Most often the white markings are edged in black. The white on the scapulars acts as a stripe on the back, and white dots persist on the upper wing coverts and flank.
- Females are similar to female buffleheads except that the brown head has three white patches instead of one, especially the round dot behind the eye.
- The wing of the female is dark brown/black and lacking white, and the male's is black with several white markings on the upper coverts and tertials. Feet of both are blue/gray.

Distribution/Habitat

- Harlequins are not an abundant duck except for a few remote areas in Alaska and along the northern West and East Coasts. They breed in Alaska and the northern Rocky Mountains, Iceland, Greenland, and northeastern Canada.
- They are common breeders and prefer habitat around fast, cold mountain streams. They do not migrate far and tend to winter along rocky coasts and feed in rough surf.

Food

- Dive in rivers and streams, often walking on bottom and feeding on aquatic insects (mayfly and stonefly nymphs, larval caddisflies), mollusks, and crustaceans.

Voice

- Quite silent, but males utter high-pitched squeals and peeps, and females utter *cek-cek-cek* calls.

Flock Information

- Fly in small flocks of 2 or 3 to maybe 10, unlike the usually large flocks of scoters and eiders that are seen. Flight is steady, fast, and low over the water.

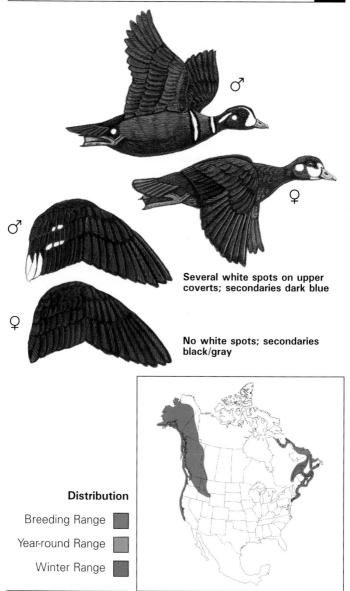

Several white spots on upper coverts; secondaries dark blue

No white spots; secondaries black/gray

Distribution

Breeding Range

Year-round Range

Winter Range

COMMON EIDER *(Somateria mollissima)*

Nicknames   Sea duck

Average Size and Weight   23″ to 26″—3½ to 6 lbs

Description

- The largest duck and one of four species of eiders in North America, the common eider has four separate races based on location and subtle plumage differences. For our purposes, just remember that the common eider along the Pacific Coast may look somewhat different than its relative on the Atlantic Coast.

- Common eider males have a pale orange bill with a long, green extension extending back almost to the eye (this extension is more rounded or pointed and helps to distinguish the four species—typically more pointed among the western species and rounded in the eastern species). Black encompasses the cap and below the eye, and pale green feathers are on the nape and behind the cheek. The neck, back, and chest are white, and the breast, belly, rump, and tail all black.

- Females are overall barred golden and dark brown with a similar membranous extension on the bill. Wings of males are black with white lesser and middle wing coverts and white tertials that curve inward. Female wings are black/brown with tan edging on the lesser and middle wing coverts and white edging on the greater secondaries and secondaries. The tertials are slightly curved.

Distribution/Habitat

- Regularly found along the coasts of the Pacific and Atlantic Flyways, common eiders breed across northern Alaska and the entire Canadian Arctic and Hudson Bay. They migrate down the coast of Alaska and along the Atlantic Coast to the northeastern states and are occasionally seen in the Great Lakes.

- They breed on the tundra and winter along rocky coastlines or open water.

Food

- Primary food is the blue mussel. Their diet is comprised totally of animal foods and includes a wide variety of mollusks and crustaceans. They feed at low tide and rest in deeper water.

Voice

- Males utter cooing sounds, and the female utters hoarse quacks.

Flock Information

- Fly in low, wavy, or loose lines, often out of sight in large seas. Flocks are 6 or 8 to a dozen or more. They are called the "B-52" of ducks because of their size, and hunters have to hit them at close ranges to make clean kills. They are difficult to hunt because of the harsh ocean conditions of late fall.

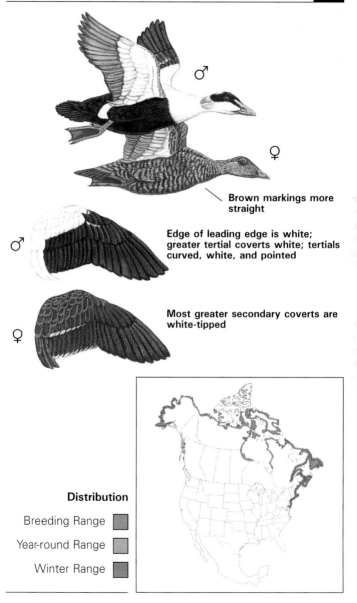

♂

♀

Brown markings more straight

Edge of leading edge is white; greater tertial coverts white; tertials curved, white, and pointed

♂

Most greater secondary coverts are white-tipped

♀

Distribution

Breeding Range

Year-round Range

Winter Range

KING EIDER *(Somateria spectabilis)*

Nicknames   Sea duck

Average Size and Weight   19″ to 25″—3 to 4 lbs

Description

- King eiders are not as numerous as common eiders but are much more numerous than the Steller's and spectacled eiders.
- The male is easily recognized by the bright orange bill and abrupt rise to an orange/yellow frontal knob outlined in black. A black line extends back from the pale green cheek to the white throat; the crown and nape are pale blue. Its neck, upper back, and chest are white, and breast, belly, sides, lower back, and rump are black; the tail is dark brown/black.
- The female and juvenile are nearly identical to the female common eider, but the common female has feathers on the sides of the bill that extend nearly to the nostrils—feathers that hardly extend forward on the female king. Female kings are brown with dark brown barring, but the barring is crescent-shaped, not straight like the common's.
- Wings of males are black with white lesser and middle wing coverts and curved black tertials with white stripes. The female's wing is dark brown and similar to the female common.

Distribution/Habitat

- King eiders breed and winter across the same areas as common eiders. They also prefer the same habitat.

Food

- Diet is similar to the common's but does include some aquatic vegetation and larval insects. Kind eiders dive to greater depths than common eiders, often exceeding 150 feet.

Voice

- Utter the same cooing and quacks of the common males and females.

Flock Information

- Similar flock formation as common eiders.

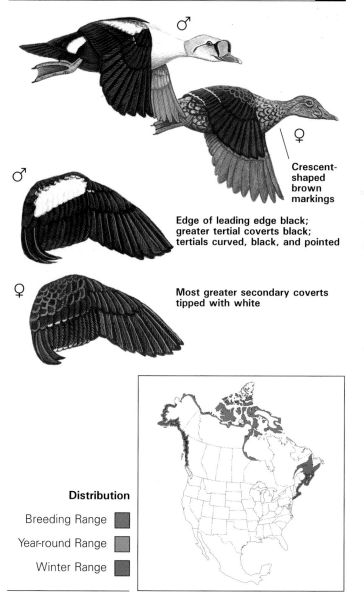

♂

♀

Crescent-shaped brown markings

♂

Edge of leading edge black; greater tertial coverts black; tertials curved, black, and pointed

♀

Most greater secondary coverts tipped with white

Distribution

Breeding Range

Year-round Range

Winter Range

STELLER'S EIDER *(Polysticta stelleri)*
SPECTACLED EIDER *(Somateria fischeri)*

Average Size and Weight Steller's: 17″ to 18″—1½ to 2½ lbs
Spectacled: 19″ to 21″—3 to 4 lbs

Description, Distribution/Habitat, Food, Flock Information

- These two eiders are the lesser known of the four North American eiders but are worth mentioning.

- Steller's eiders are the smallest of the four and the most ducklike in appearance. The male has a white head with green spots in front and behind the eye. A black spot sits on the nape, and the chin and neck are collared in black. A black spot sits on the side of the upper neck; a black band runs down the back, and white borders it and the rust sides and breast. The rump, tail coverts, and tail are brown/black. Long scapulars are blue, black, and white; the upper coverts are white and tertials curved.

- The Steller's eider hen is overall brown with dark brown mottling, and both sexes have a blue speculum that is edged front and back with white.

- The male spectacled eider has an orange bill with green feathers extending down the bill to the nostrils. The eye is surrounded by white lined with black, and the nape is green. The chin, neck, and most of the back are white, while the rump, tail, sides, chest, and belly are all black.

- Spectacled females are brown with similar brown feathers to the nostrils and a pale eye patch; otherwise they have similar brown mottling as other female eiders. Both sexes have pale blue eyes.

- Both species in North America are restricted to the coastal waters of Alaska and the Bering Sea; consequently, most people never get to see or hunt them. Their foods are similar to the other eiders. Steller's are the smallest and fastest of all four species.

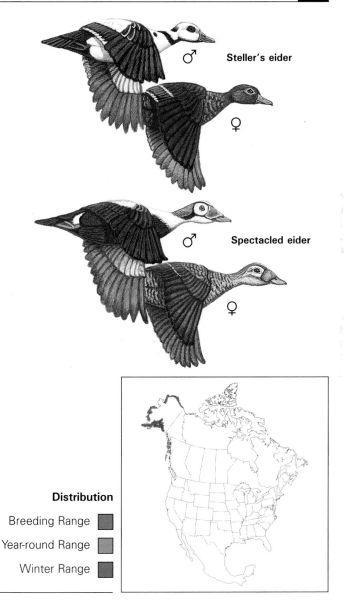

Steller's eider ♂

♀

Spectacled eider ♂

♀

Distribution

Breeding Range

Year-round Range

Winter Range

BLACK SCOTER *(Melanitta nigra)*

Nicknames   Coot, Black coot, Common scoter

Average Size and Weight   17″ to 20″—2 to 3 lbs

Description
- Three species of scoters occupy North America: black, surf, and white-winged. The black scoter was so named for the black plumage and lack of any white on the entire body of the male. Males have a black bill and bright yellow/orange knob at the base, and some have slight gray underwings, otherwise, a totally black body and wings.
- Females are overall dark brown with a dark crown and light face, chin, and throat. The bill is black, and feet of both sexes are dark gray; their heads are round.
- The wings can be used to identify sex by examining the ninth and tenth primaries. The last 50 or 60 millimeters of the inner vane of the tenth primary of the male is attenuated; the female's is not attenuated but is narrower and shorter.

Distribution/Habitat
- Black scoters breed across portions of Alaska and northcentral and northeastern Canada and winter along both coasts, as well as frequenting the Great Lakes.
- They prefer large ponds, freshwater lakes, and coastal bays.

Food
- Their primary food is the blue mussel, but they also feed on other mollusks and crustaceans, insect larvae, and some aquatic vegetation. They typically feed in 20 to 30 feet of water.

Voice
- Both sexes utter *cor-loo* calls and other cries.

Flock Information
- They, like the other sea ducks, seldom fly over land. Flight is steady, and flocks of 2 or 3 to 1 or 2 dozen fly in loose, wavering lines low to the water.

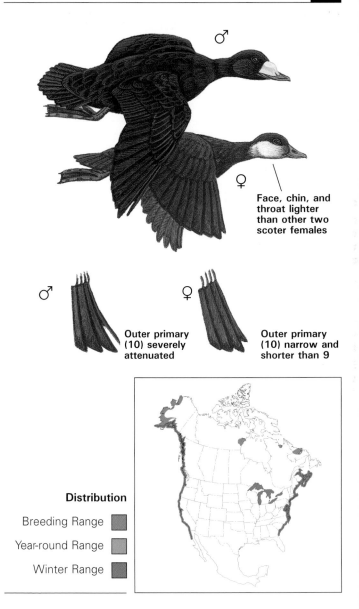

♂

♀

Face, chin, and throat lighter than other two scoter females

♂ Outer primary (10) severely attenuated

♀ Outer primary (10) narrow and shorter than 9

Distribution

Breeding Range

Year-round Range

Winter Range

SURF SCOTER *(Melanitta perspicillata)*

Nicknames   Coot, Sea coot, Skunkhead

Average Size and Weight   18″ to 21″—1½ to 2½ lbs

Description

- The surf scoter, so named for being found near or at the breaking waves and surf, is all black like the black scoter except for the two white marks on the forehead and back of the head. The head is more sloped than the black scoter; the bill has a black hump on top, a black spot at the lower base surrounded by red/orange at the rear and top and white in front, and the rest of the bill is orange/yellow. Its eyes are white/pale blue and the feet orange.
- Females are overall brown with a similarly shaped gray bill having a large black spot at the base; the eye is brown. The head is likewise sloped, with two lighter patches on each side of the face and a light patch on the nape. Its underside may be lighter than the rest of the body and its feet pink/yellow.
- To sex these birds, look for the black wings of males and dark brown wings of females. Males tend to have longer and more pointed tertials that extend below the level of the secondaries more than on the female. Both sexes can be determined from the black scoter wing by examining the tenth primary—it is as long or longer than the ninth.

Distribution/Habitat

- Surf scoters breed in the open boreal forest of northern Canada and Alaska. They winter along each coast, a portion of the southeastern Gulf States, and parts of the Great Lakes.
- They prefer smaller, woodland ponds, lakes, and rivers, and winter on large coastal waters and large inland lakes.

Food

- Surf scoters feed in similar depths and on similar foods as that of the black scoter, often at the line of surf or breaking waves.

Voice

- Rarely vocal.

Flock Information

- Flocks are similar in size to those of the black scoter but fly in more regular formation than white-winged scoters. Wings make a whistling sound that isn't quite as distinct as the goldeneye.

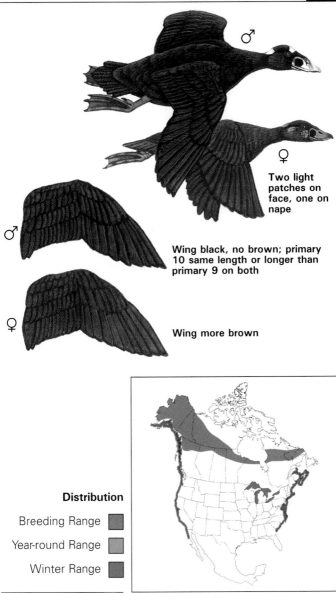

♂

♀

Two light patches on face, one on nape

♂

Wing black, no brown; primary 10 same length or longer than primary 9 on both

♀

Wing more brown

Distribution

Breeding Range

Year-round Range

Winter Range

WHITE-WINGED SCOTER *(Melanitta fusca)*

Nicknames   Coot, Sea coot, Whitewing

Average Size and Weight   19″ to 23″—2½ to 4 lbs

Description

- White-winged scoters are bigger than the other two scoters and the only one with white on their wings. The body of the male is black like the other two, and variations occur only on the head and wings. The bill is an orange/red color with a black knob at the upper base; a small white crescent sits below and behind the pale blue/white eye. The feet of both sexes are pink.

- The female is overall dark brown like the other female scoters and has a gray bill and two light gray patches on the head—one in front and one behind the brown eye.

- Wings of both sexes have a white speculum, and the rest of the feathers are black on males and dark brown on females. The tips of the greater secondary coverts are white on each; the tips on the male's wing appear as diagonals, whereas the tips on the female's wing appear as a straight line.

Distribution/Habitat

- Whitewings breed across much of Alaska and northcentral and northwestern Canada and winter along both coasts and the Great Lakes.

- They prefer woodland lakes and marshes for breeding and large coastal waters and large inland lakes during the winter.

Food

- Feed on similar foods as the other scoters—blue mussels, clams, and a wide variety of other mollusks and crustaceans. They dive up to 80 or 90 feet for food but typically feed in 20 feet of water.

Voice

- Rarely vocal but may utter whistling notes.

Flock Information

- Flight is similar to the other scoters, but the lines are more wavy and irregular.

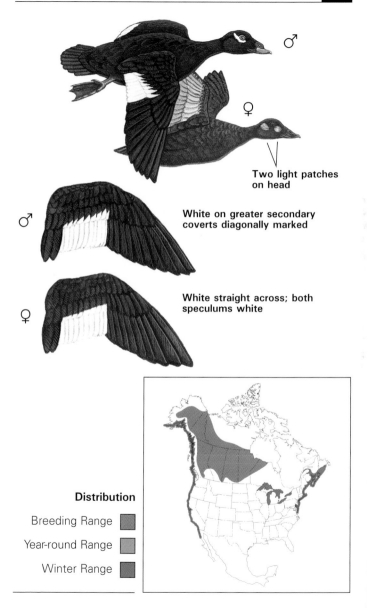

♂

♀

Two light patches
on head

White on greater secondary
coverts diagonally marked

♂

♀

White straight across; both
speculums white

Distribution

Breeding Range

Year-round Range

Winter Range

Geese and Swans

GREATER WHITE-FRONTED GOOSE
(Anser albifrons)

Nicknames   Specklebelly, Speck, Whitefront, Laughing goose

Average Size and Weight   27″ to 29″ — 5 to 6½ lbs

Description

- The white-fronted goose is commonly referred to by two other descriptive nicknames, "specklebelly" (speck) or "whitefront." A large white frontal face patch gives it its common name, with a brown head and pink/orange bill. The body is overall brown/ gray, and the legs and feet are pink. The light gray breast on adults is blotched and barred with black/brown markings, giving it the nickname "specklebelly."
- Sexes are similar, as with all geese, but immatures lack the white face patch and barring and are noticeably smaller.

Distribution/Habitat

- Specks are found throughout the Central and Pacific Flyways, with breeding occurring in Alaska and much of the northwestern Arctic. On breeding grounds, they are found on low tundra near water. During migration many stops are made to feed on wheat, pea, and other grain fields of the Canadian prairies and upper Midwest. They winter in salt marshes on the Gulf Coast. Migration typically begins early in September.

Food

- Grasses and grains—corn, wheat, lentils, peas, etc. It's often said that once a speck gets in the peas, he won't come out until they're gone!

Voice

- Main call a higher-pitched *kow-yow* or *kay-yow-wow*, and a flock of specks calling sounds like human laughter.

Flock Information

- Flocks of several to several hundred or more specks fly in the "V" formation of Canada geese. Their call is often the first sign of specks in the area.

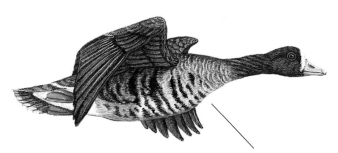

Black barring present on adults, lacking on juveniles

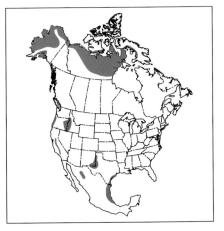

Distribution

Breeding Range

Year-round Range

Winter Range

LESSER SNOW GOOSE *(Chen caerulescens)*
ROSS' GOOSE *(Chen rossii)*

Nicknames Lesser snow: Snow, Blue, White goose, Waive
Ross': Snow, Warty nose, Waive

Average Size and Weight 28″ to 29″ — 5 to 6½ lbs
23″ to 25″ — 3 to 4 lbs

Description

- Snow geese appear in two color phases: blue and white. Both are the same species, though, and the blue phase should not be referred to as "blue goose." Snows are bigger than the smaller Ross' goose, which have light pink feet and a shorter, stubbier bill with a warty base that lacks the typical grinning patch of the snow goose; Ross' exhibit a blue phase, although it is not as common as the blue phase of the snow goose. Snows have scarlet feet and a longer bill with a characteristic black grinning patch. In both species, the primaries of the white wings are black.

- Juveniles of both species are white and gray. Their bills and legs are gray. The head, breast, and belly of snow and Ross' are often stained with a brown/copper color from iron in the water and soil where they feed.

Distribution/Habitat

- The continental population of lesser snow geese is currently in serious trouble due to an overabundance of birds; increased hunting seasons and bag limits have not significantly helped reduce the numbers, and it is feared the population may crash soon.

- Snow geese are highly gregarious, often seen in enormous flocks numbering in the thousands. Snows breed on the tundra of Hudson Bay and west throughout the Arctic. They begin leaving in September for wintering grounds in the Gulf States of Louisiana and Texas. Snows can be found in all flyways, but the biggest concentrations are seen in the Mississippi and Central Flyways.

- Once not as plentiful, Ross' breed across much of the same range as the snows and winter along the Gulf, with highest concentrations in Texas.

Food

- Feed on aquatic roots and tubers, grubbed up from moist soils and pools, as well as the succulent shoots of many grains. Crop damage from large feeding flocks is a problem for many farmers.

Voice

- Most vocal of all waterfowl, gabbling a constant *low ow-ow-ow* or high-pitched cry resembling dogs barking. Ross' geese make similar but higher pitched sounds.

Flock Information

- On staging grounds in Canada, snows and Ross' fly in smaller groups, but flocks of hundreds and thousands are normal during migration. Formations are staggered U-shaped or crescent-shaped lines—not tight formations like Canada geese.

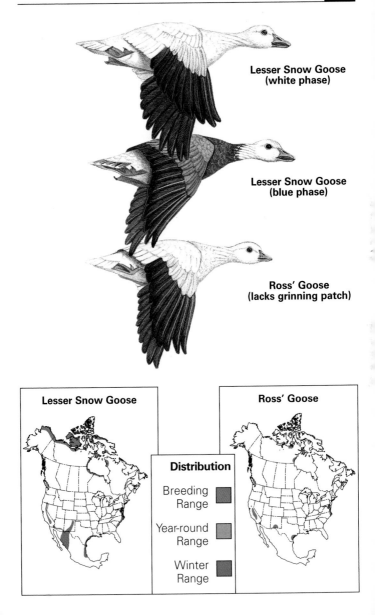

Lesser Snow Goose
(white phase)

Lesser Snow Goose
(blue phase)

Ross' Goose
(lacks grinning patch)

Lesser Snow Goose

Ross' Goose

Distribution

Breeding
Range

Year-round
Range

Winter
Range

CANADA GOOSE *(Branta canadensis)*

Nicknames   Honker, Canada

Average Size and Weight   Eleven subspecies exist in North America, ranging
in size and weight from the smallest, 23″ and 3 lbs,
to the largest, 42″ and 11 to 15 lbs

Description

• Canada geese are the most common and identifiable goose. The head and neck are
long, with a notable white face patch. Bill, legs, and feet are also black. The black
rump has a white V, and the undertail coverts and belly are white. The wings and
back are dark brown, and the breast feathers are dark to light gray with buff tips.
Sexes are similar.

Distribution/Habitat

• Abundant in all four flyways, Canada geese breed throughout all of Canada and into
Alaska and winter in many of the central to southern states and even into Mexico.
Many Canadas—incorrectly referred to as Canadians—have taken up residency
in cities or rural areas, becoming pests on golf courses and lawns. Early September nuisance hunting seasons take place in many states to help control the local
populations.

• Canadas are found on large and small lakes, ponds, marshes, and rivers. They feed
in agricultural fields, often making morning and evening trips from resting water to
fields.

Food

• Tip up to feed on aquatic plants, and crops of corn, wheat, peas, alfalfa, etc.

Voice

• Recognizable and resonant *her-honk!* and series of honks and other lower gabbles
—very vocal.

Flock Information

• Flocks are smaller than snow geese, ranging from family flocks of 5 to 8 to migrating flocks of 50 to 100 or more. Typical formation is a "V" shape.

Distribution

Breeding Range �+ ☐

Year-round Range ☐

Winter Range ■

BRANT *(Branta bernicla)*

Nicknames   Sea goose, Black brant, Atlantic brant

Average Size and Weight   23″ to 24″ — 2½ to 3½ lbs

Description

- Brant were formerly divided into two species, the Atlantic and Pacific (black) brant. They are now considered one species with two subspecies: *nigricans* (Pacific) and *brota* (Atlantic). Small geese, they can only be confused with the Canada goose along the coasts.
- Both subspecies have a black head, neck, chest, and breast, with dark wings and tail. Lower breast and sides are light gray to white, with darker streaking, and belly and undertail are white. The *nigricans* has a pronounced white crescent shape on the sides of the neck, while this is not nearly as pronounced on the *brota*.
- Sexes are similar.

Distribution/Habitat

- Brant are a saltwater bird and found along both coasts, inland bays, and brackish water. The Pacific species breeds on the Alaskan coast and Yukon and winters along the coasts of Mexico and the Baja Peninsula. The Atlantic species breeds in the central Canadian Arctic and works its way south to the Carolinas. Found along the coast in bays and estuaries, following the tides where food is exposed.

Food

- Feed on many species of algae, sedge, aquatic plants, sea lettuce, and eelgrass.

Voice

- As the other geese, brant are quite vocal. Call is a low *cronk-cronk* or *ruk-ruk*.

Flock Information

- Fly in low, loose flocks of wavy lines—no established formation. Wingbeats are much more rapid than the deliberate strokes of the Canada goose.

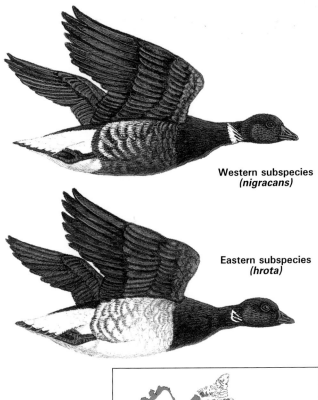

Western subspecies
(nigracans)

Eastern subspecies
(hrota)

Distribution

Breeding Range

Year-round Range

Winter Range

TUNDRA SWAN *(Cygnus columbianus)*
MUTE SWAN *(Cygnus olor)*
TRUMPETER SWAN *(Cygnus buccinator)*

Nicknames	Tundra: Whistling swan
	Mute: Common swan, Royal swan
	Trumpeter: Bugler swan, Wild swan
Average Size and Weight	Tundra: 52″ — 12 to 17 lbs
	Mute: 58″ — 21 to 25 lbs
	Trumpeter: 58″ — 23 to 29 lbs

Description

- The three North American swans are tundra, mute, and trumpeter. Their long necks, white wingtips, and black legs and feet distinguish them from the smaller snow goose.
- Tundra swans, formerly called whistling swans, are the only legal game bird in a handful of states. At rest, the neck is straighter than the curved neck of the mute swan. Typically, there is a yellow mark below the eye, and the black skin narrowing from the bill to the eye does not encompass as much of the eye as on the trumpeter swan.
- Mute swans have orange bills bordered by a black, fleshy base and black knob on the forehead. Their wings make a loud *woosh* sound in flight.
- Trumpeters are the largest North American waterfowl, with the head and neck the length of the rest of the body. Similar to the tundra swan except for size and black skin extending over more of the eye. Its forehead is more sloped than the other two species.
- Adult male swans are called cobs, adult females are pens, and young are called cygnets. Juveniles are a dull gray or light brown, and sexes are similar, but adult males tend to be bigger than females.

Distribution/Habitat

- Tundra swans breed on tundra and migrate down both coasts to winter in the southern Rockies, Texas, and Southwest. Mute swans are primarily found in the Great Lakes states and east to the coast. Trumpeter swans, once almost extinct, are now found from Alaska throughout parts of central Canada and the northwestern United States.
- Habitat includes small ponds, marshes (fresh and salt), lakes, and rivers.

Food

- Tip up to feed on aquatic vegetation, invertebrates, and mollusks. Trumpeters often use their feet to clear mud to expose roots and stems. Tundra and mute swans, like geese, often feed in fields on waste grain.

Voice

- Mute swans are quite silent; however, the tundra emits higher-pitched whistles—*kow-wow-kow*—than the lower, more bugling sound of the trumpeter's *koo-hoo*.

Flock Information

- Fly in typical "V" formation like Canada geese, especially tundra swans during migration. Mute and trumpeter swans are typically seen in pairs or small family groups.

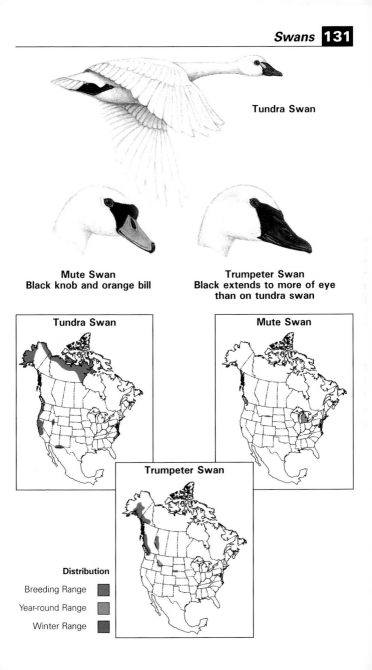

Tundra Swan

Mute Swan
Black knob and orange bill

Trumpeter Swan
Black extends to more of eye
than on tundra swan

Tundra Swan

Mute Swan

Trumpeter Swan

Distribution

Breeding Range

Year-round Range

Winter Range

Other Birds

SANDHILL CRANE (*Grus canadensis*)

Average Size   37″ to 44″

Description

- Sandhill cranes resemble herons and other long-legged marsh birds, not the ducks and geese of this book. The bill is long and pointed, crown red, and cheek and throat white. The nape, long neck, and entire body is gray, with large feathers covering the rump. Often the feathers are tinged with brown or rust from iron in the water and soil where they feed.

- They are common across most of Canada and many parts of the northern United States, often wintering in the extreme southern United States. Primary habitat is shallow marshes or half-dried wetlands, pastures, or shallow rivers with islands. They feed on seeds and shoots of many plants, and during migration, gather in large flocks to feed on grain in agricultural fields. They are a game bird in a number of states and hunted like geese. Be careful, though—crippled cranes have been known to use their spearlike bills to hurt or even kill dogs sent to retrieve them.

- Sandhills have a visual mating dance involving the male and female dancing toward one another. Their call is a loud, hoarse *crrroooak* audible at a good distance.

Feathers often
tinged with rust
from ferrous soils
and water

Distribution

Breeding Range ▮

Year-round Range ▮

Winter Range ▮

AMERICAN COOT *(Fulica americana)*

Average Size   14″

Description

- The coot is a marsh bird that is a common sight anywhere ducks are found. They are small and gray, with a black head, red eye, and large frontal "shield" rising from the white bill; a black stripe circles the tip. A white rump and white edging on the secondaries are the only white feathers on the entire body. The yellow/green feet are lobed and not webbed, which aids in walking on light vegetation but still allows efficient swimming.

- Coots are common across the whole continent and very prolific. Many potholes in the prairie pothole region are filled to the hilt with coots. Between their beeps, clucks, splashing and diving, they make a great deal of commotion, and there are few noisier places than a spring marsh loaded with coots. Coots feed mostly on aquatic vegetation as well as some insects or invertebrates.

- Flight is not their forté, so they prefer to swim or dive to evade danger. They need a long, running start to get airborne, and their legs dangle out behind. Most hunters do not pursue them, but often in the south, hunters pole boats through vegetation and shoot them on the flush. The meat is supposed to be quite good.

Feet lobed

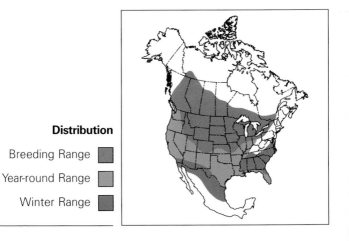

Distribution

Breeding Range

Year-round Range

Winter Range

COMMON MOORHEN *(Gallinula chloropus)*

Average Size   13″

Description
- Moorhens are often confused with the coot, but their overall size is smaller and their bill is red with yellow tip and red frontal shield instead of white. The feet are not lobed, and the white lines along the sides help to distinguish it from the coot and purple gallinule.
- Found in the eastern United States on the shores and shallows of marshes or ponds, where they feed mainly on aquatic vegetation. Not commonly seen by hunters, but some jumpshoot them from a poled boat.

PURPLE GALLINULE *(Porphyrula martinica)*

Average Size   12″

Description
- Smaller yet than the moorhen, the purple gallinule is purple on the head, neck, chest, breast, and belly; the bill is thick red with a yellow tip. The frontal shield is a pale blue; purple graduates into a green back, sides, rump, and wings. Undertail coverts are white. The long legs and oversized feet are yellow. Juveniles are overall brown.
- They are primarily found in the southeastern United States in fresh or saltwater ponds, marshes, and swamps with much floating vegetation. They feed on aquatic plants and insects. Their light weight and large feet allow them to run along the tops of large floating plants, such as water hyacinth.

Common moorhen

Purple gallinule

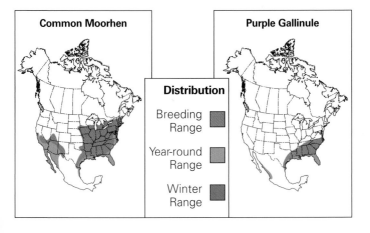

Common Moorhen

Purple Gallinule

Distribution

Breeding Range

Year-round Range

Winter Range

VIRGINIA RAIL *(Rallus limicola)*

Average Size   10″

Description

- The Virginia rail is an overall rust-colored marsh bird with a long, orange/black bill, dark crown, gray cheeks, and dark barring on the flanks. Wings are rusty/chestnut, legs are red, and the rump is white.
- They are common across most of the United States and prefer moderately vegetated marshes or wetlands, feeding on invertebrates. They swim and scoot through cover. Call is a *kick-a-kick-a.*

KING RAIL *(Rallus elegans)*

Average Size   17″

Description

- King rails are much larger than Virginia rails, with long red/black bills that curve downward slightly at the end. The head is dark on top with gray cheeks, light stripe over the eye, and white throat. The neck, chest, and wings are rust/chestnut, and the flanks are barred black and white. The feathers on the back are black with tan edging, a characteristic that helps distinguish it from the clapper rail.
- They are found in the eastern United States and along the Atlantic Coast in fresh and saltwater marshes. Food is comprised of crustaceans, aquatic invertebrates, aquatic plants, seeds, and a variety of other similar foods. Often confused with the clapper rail when hunting. A variety of calls center around the basic *kik-kik-kik* sound heard by clapper rails.

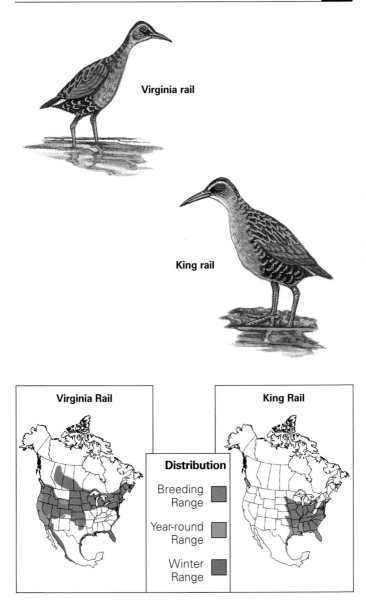

Virginia rail

King rail

Virginia Rail

King Rail

Distribution

Breeding Range

Year-round Range

Winter Range

CLAPPER RAIL *(Rallus longirostris)*

Average Size   15″

Description

- Clapper rails have a bill that is similar to the king rail, with a dark crown, gray cheek and white throat. The chest and belly are pale and light brown/gray, and the brown feathers on the back are edged in gray, not tan, as in the king rail. The sides and flanks are barred with white, and the legs are gray/pink.
- Clapper rails are found along the Atlantic, Gulf, and southern Pacific Coasts in coastal salt marshes. Foods and calls are similar to the king rail. Clapper rails are hunted along the coast by hunters who take turns pushing one another through weeds in a skiff or boat until these birds jump in a low, gangly flight.

SORA *(Porzana carolina)*

Average Size   9″

Description

- The sora is the most abundant and common rail in North America. Its short, thick bill is yellow, and a black face and throat patch are common identifiers. The crown is rusty/brown and the cheek, neck, and chest are gray. The nape and upper back are brown/olive, and the back is mottled with black, brown, and white, with an overall olive tint. The sides are barred with dark brown and white, and the undertail coverts are white; its short legs are yellow/green.
- Soras are found throughout the United States, Canada, and Mexico in marshes and lakes with good amounts of thick vegetation. They mainly eat seeds and leaves of aquatic plants, such as smartweed, duckweed, sedges, and a variety of others, as well as insects and mollusks. Call is a higher-pitched *er-wee*.

Clapper rail

Sora

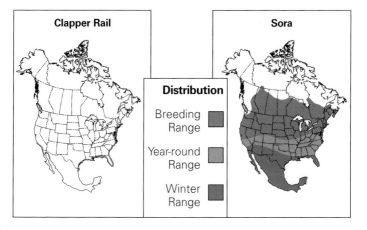

North American Flyways

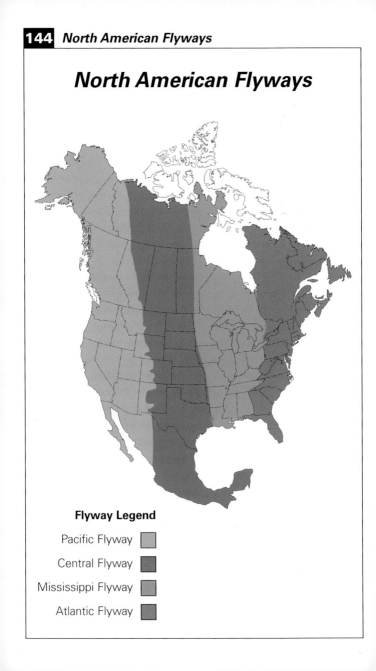

Flyway Legend

Pacific Flyway

Central Flyway

Mississippi Flyway

Atlantic Flyway

North American Flyways

THE WATERFOWL OF NORTH AMERICA are mostly migratory, with the exception of isolated, resident populations of ducks or geese that seem to live in one area year-round. These birds follow quite specific migration corridors, or flyways, each year as the weather and daylight change—most movements are north to south and south to north again, but they often include east to west and west to east movements.

Many of these birds are found only in certain flyways, and knowing which flyway you're in and what birds are there is the first clue to identifying the duck or goose being observed. North America is divided up into four major flyways—the Pacific, Central, Mississippi, and Atlantic. The Pacific Flyway encompasses the entire West Coast, from the Bering Straight to the western coast of Mexico. The Central Flyway covers much of the central region of the Canadian provinces and United States, such as Saskatchewan, Manitoba, the Dakotas, Kansas, and Texas. The Mississippi Flyway largely follows the Mississippi River system, a traditional migration artery, and the Atlantic Flyway covers the entire East Coast and some distance inland.

There is a fair amount of overlap in flyways, so some birds typically found in one flyway are often found in another, and many are found in two, three, or all four. Even in rare cases, where one bird has never been spotted in a particular flyway, it can turn up there, so there are no absolutes. But the flyway system has been well documented and studied over many years and is a helpful tool in determining the identity of a species.

One important region ducks depend on are the prairie pothole areas of the southcentral Canadian prairies and northcentral United States. This region is full of wetlands and associated vegetative cover, offering excellent nesting and brood rearing habitat, especially in wet years. The abundance of water and food make this region responsible for more than 50 percent of the continent's waterfowl production.

In the years of abundant water, such as the mid to late 1990s, duck reproduction in the prairie potholes is at an all time high, and many species are experiencing tremendous growth. Without this "duck factory," many duck populations would not be what they are today. However, without the work of many organizations, duck numbers would have suffered over the years. Organizations such as Ducks Unlimited and Delta Waterfowl raise money and volunteer time to help create, set aside, and preserve places like the prairie potholes and other wetlands and nesting habitat necessary to waterfowl.

Flyway Appendix

THIS APPENDIX SERVES as a quick guide to the species found in each flyway instead of looking up the distribution map for each bird in the main text. If you simply want to know whether you could expect to see a black duck on your South Dakota pothole, you would look up black duck below and note that it is common in the Atlantic Flyway, uncommon in the Mississippi Flyway, and only rare in the Central. You would conclude, then, that a bird approaching that looks like a mallard is probably going to be a mallard, since mallards are extremely common in the Central Flyway and black ducks are only rare at best.

Next to each bird is a letter or several letters that correspond to the flyways in which you might encounter each bird: "P" is for Pacific, "C" is for Central, "M" is for Mississippi, and "A" is for Atlantic. A capital letter means the bird is common to extremely common in that flyway; a lowercase letter means the bird is present but not common; a lowercase letter in parenthesis ( ) means the bird is rarely found in that flyway; and no letter means you should not expect to see it at all in that flyway.

An example would be:

Black Duck . . . .(c), m, A

This means the black duck is commonly found in the Atlantic Flyway, uncommonly found in the Mississippi Flyway, rarely in the Central, and not at all in the Pacific.

Waterfowl Flyway Key

PUDDLE DUCKS

American Black Duck	(c), m, A
American Wigeon	P, C, M, a
Black-bellied Whistling Duck	(p), c
Blue-winged Teal	p, C, M, a
Cinnamon Teal	P, c
Fulvous Whistling Duck	p, c
Gadwall	p, C, M, a
Green-winged Teal	P, C, M, a
Mallard	P, C, M, A
Mottled Duck	m, a
Northern Pintail	P, C, m, a
Northern Shoveler	P, C, m, a
Wood Duck	p, c, M, A

DIVING DUCKS

Barrow's Goldeneye	P, c, a
Black Scoter	P, (m), A
Bufflehead	P, c, M, A
Canvasback	P, C, M, A
Common Eider	P, A
Common Goldeneye	P, C, M, A
Common Merganser	P, C, M, A
Greater Scaup	P, (c), m, A
Harlequin Duck	P, c, a
Hooded Merganser	P, c, M, A
King Eider	P, A
Lesser Scaup	P, C, M, A
Oldsquaw	P, (c), m, A
Red-breasted Merganser	P, (c), (m), A
Redhead	P, C, M, a
Ring-necked Duck	p, c, M, a
Ruddy Duck	P, C, m, a
Spectacled Eider	p

Steller's Eider . . . . p
Surf Scoter . . . . P, c, (m), a
White-winged Scoter . . . . P, C, (m), a

GEESE AND SWANS

Brant . . . . P, A
Canada Goose . . . . P, C, M, A
Greater White-fronted Goose . . . . p, C, m
Lesser Snow Goose . . . . P, C, M, a
Mute Swan . . . . (p), (c), M, a
Ross' Goose . . . . P, C, m, (a)
Trumpeter Swan . . . . p, (c)
Tundra Swan . . . . p, C, M, a

OTHER BIRDS

American Coot . . . . P, C, M, A
Clapper Rail . . . . p, m, a
Common Moorhen . . . . p, c, M, A
King Rail . . . . (c), M, A
Purple Gallinule . . . . (c), m, a
Sandhill Crane . . . . p, C, M, (a)
Sora . . . . P, C, M, A
Virginia Rail . . . . P, C, M, A

Bird Species Observation List

Upland Birds

BIRD	DATE / LOCATION
American Woodcock	
Blue Grouse	
Chukar	
Common Snipe	
Eastern Wild Turkey	
Florida (Osceola) Turkey	
Gambel's Quail	
Gould's Turkey	
Gray (Hungarian) Partridge	
Greater Prairie Chicken	
Merriam's Turkey	
Montezuma (Mearns') Quail	
Mountain Quail	
Mourning Dove	
Northern Bobwhite Quail	
Ring-necked Pheasant	
Rio Grande Turkey	
Rock Ptarmigan	
Ruffed Grouse	
Sage Grouse	
Scaled Quail	
Sharp-tailed Grouse	

BIRD	DATE / LOCATION
Spruce Grouse	
Valley Quail	
White-tailed Ptarmigan	
White-winged Dove	
Willow Ptarmigan	

Puddle Ducks

American Black Duck	
American Wigeon	
Black-bellied Whistling Duck	
Blue-winged Teal	
Cinnamon Teal	
Fulvous Whistling Duck	
Gadwall	
Green-winged Teal	
Mallard	
Mottled Duck	
Northern Pintail	
Northern Shoveler	
Wood Duck	

Diving Ducks

Barrow's Goldeneye	
Black Scoter	
Bufflehead	
Canvasback	

BIRD	DATE / LOCATION
Common Eider	
Common Goldeneye	
Common Merganser	
Greater Scaup	
Harlequin Duck	
Hooded Merganser	
King Eider	
Lesser Scaup	
Oldsquaw	
Red-breasted Merganser	
Redhead	
Ring-necked Duck	
Ruddy Duck	
Spectacled Eider	
Steller's Eider	
Surf Scoter	
White-winged Scoter	

Geese and Swans

Brant	
Canada Goose	
Greater White-fronted Goose	
Lesser Snow Goose	
Mute Swan	
Ross' Goose	
Trumpeter Swan	
Tundra Swan	

Other Birds

BIRD	DATE / LOCATION
American Coot	
Clapper Rail	
Common Moorhen	
King Rail	
Purple Gallinule	
Sandhill Crane	
Sora	
Virginia Rail	

Christopher Smith
Wildlife and Sporting Dog Artist

Christopher Smith is a wildlife artist from northern Michigan. He specializes in dogs and wildlife scenes, which he executes for pet owners and wildlife lovers across the country.

Smith has illustrated more than a dozen hunting and fishing books. He is the Contributing Artist for *The Retriever Journal* and a freelance illustrator for *The Pointing Dog Journal* and *Shooting Sportsman*. He, along with brother Jason, is co-author of *Waterfowling Horizons*, a hardcover book about modern waterfowl hunting.

Smith is a graduate of Lake Superior State University in Sault Ste. Marie, MI, holding a B.S. in Fisheries and Wildlife Management. He and wife, Lani, an artist and potter, are overrun by obnoxious Labradors in their northern Michigan home. He has hunted, fished, and bird-watched across much of North America, adding hands-on experiences to his formal education in the wildlife sciences.